THE MEANING OF HOLINESS

D1106949

3/23

THE MEANING OF
HOLINESS

by

LOUIS LAVELLE

PANTHEON BOOKS INC.
NEW YORK
1954

This translation of Quatre Saints (*A. Michel, Paris,* 1951)
was made by
DOROTHEA O'SULLIVAN

NIHIL OBSTAT: RICARDVS ROCHE, S.T.D.
CENSOR DEPVTATVS
IMPRIMATVR: ✠ HVMPHREY BRIGHT
EPISCOPVS TITVLARIS SOLENSIS
VICARIVS CAPITVLARIS BIRMINGAMIENSIS
BIRMINGAMIAE: DIE VI MAII MCMLIV

PRINTED IN GREAT BRITAIN

CONTENTS

Contents

I

ON HOLINESS

I. THE SAINTS IN OUR MIDST

THERE are saints among us. But we often fail to recognize them. It is hard to believe they can inhabit this world of ours. They all seem to have left it behind. We invoke them as though they were all in heaven and able to bestow on us only invisible and supernatural favours. It would seem to be presumption on our part to seek to imitate them. Our Christian name serves rarely to remind us of the protection the saints are able to afford, now that they have become ministers of God and dispensers of His gifts. Yet it is their death that has made them saints; for it was death that brought about the spiritual transformation without which they would be mere men like ourselves. They are now so purified as to seem mere symbols of the virtue which marked their life and which is active in us by force of an example we can never hope to equal. It seems ridiculous that someone whom we have seen and touched, whose weaknesses, foibles and faults we have observed, whose life has been involved in our life and whose brow was adorned by no halo, should have trod the path of holiness before our eyes without our having any inkling of it. But holiness is invisible alike on earth and in heaven; and it is far more difficult to identify under the appearances of flesh and blood than in its conceptual form as an image or an idea.

Yet a saint is not pure spirit. He may not be mistaken for an angel: even death cannot make him one. For holiness belongs primarily to this world. It bears witness that the life we live on earth, a bodily life with all its weakness and pettiness, is yet capable of receiving the rays of supernatural light and of taking on a new and transcendent meaning. This teaches us not merely to endure life, but to desire and even to love it. We are apt to think of a saint as an exceptional being, who has decided to live apart from everyday life, and no longer shares its wretchedness—in fact as one who lives in communion with God and out of communion with us. But this is not true. Precisely because he lives in communion with God, the saint is the one man who is in communion with us, while all other men live to some extent apart.

No outward sign marks off the saint from any passer-by who fails to attract our notice. To all appearance he lives the life of Everyman. We see him intent on his allotted task and never seeming to be diverted from it. He never refuses any work that he is invited to undertake: each successive event is an opportunity to be used. He is interested in each and all of us so spontaneously and naturally, that he seems simply to enlarge the society to which we belong. We do not find, as we should have expected, that he has renounced his human nature or overcome and eradicated his faults of character. He can still be angry and violent, and a prey to passion. He does not seek, as so many do, to disguise those passions. But to see him give way to passion is for us something of a scandal which prevents our thinking of him as a saint and often inclines us to set ourselves above him. One may say indeed that he mortifies his passions, but they remain a condition and even an element of his holiness. For holiness is itself a passion; or if the phrase offends us, let us call it a sublimated passion. There is in passion a power which holiness needs in order to break away from prejudice and habit. Passion always has its roots in the body; it is passion which stimulates and raises the body to higher levels of living. There is nothing finer than to see the fire which feeds on the most base materials produce at its highest point a flame radiating so great a light.

2. THE SAINT ALWAYS GOES TO THE LIMIT
OF HIS POWERS

In every one of our neighbours there is a potential saint. He may not necessarily become one, for there is also in him a potential criminal or even a potential devil. And the agony of mind which is a characteristic of our time (the majority of the moderns seek to identify it with consciousness itself) is a token of our uncertainty as to which of these potentialities will in the long run prevail. The Jansenists knew such agony of mind. But on the whole men are content with a mediocre existence, with a round of merely commonplace tasks and temporal interests. The mark of the saint is that he always lives at the limit of his powers. There is no one whose life is so close to the spontaneous movements of nature. He seems in a way to surrender to them, to find in them the source and spring of all his action. We may indeed think that he fights against these natural impulses; but it would be more true to say that he directs them all to their final end, to the point at which they bring him perfect satisfaction and fulfilment. In the process he is obliged to transcend the limits of nature, in order that nature may achieve in him the end towards which it aspires. In like manner one sees the mathematician, using the concept of limit, press to infinity a series of terms and so transcend the concept he is using. So too the saint never brings into play and never suggests the use of any save the most familiar sentiments. No one is more accessible than he. But of these same sentiments he makes a most extraordinary use; for he manages to give them their full power only by forcing them (in order to fulfil their aspiration) to transcend the uses to which we had previously consecrated them. At the moment when they seem to approach fulfilment, they appear to give way or to be transformed into something of a wholly different order. And so in the

saint we recognize all the impulses of nature, and yet in a
sense we do not. It would be a mistake to think of him as
always engaged in a relentless war against his natural impulses,
for nature also comes from God. He transforms nature into
the supernatural. He rediscovers its origin, its destiny and its
full significance. It is easy to understand how one who remains caught up in the toils of nature is bound to debase and
degrade the powers which nature has put at his disposal. For
both the divine and the diabolical contain the same elements.
A slight inflection of our freedom suffices to turn the one
into the other. It is in the life of the spirit that the life of
nature finds its true fulfilment. It is to misread nature not to
see that nature is itself a figure. Immanence is shorn of all
its value if we are content to rest in it, and if we fail to see
that in transcendence it has its origin and its end; and that
in this same transcendence it finds a fleeting and precarious
approach to that of which death alone can give possession
and fulfilment.

3. THE SAINT IS INDIFFERENT TO HIS HUMAN SITUATION

The mark of holiness is to lay bare to us the relation
between two worlds, the material and the spiritual; or again,
to show that there is in truth only one world with two faces,
one luminous and one obscure. By the outward appearance
of this world (in which our transient being has a share), we
may allow ourselves to be deceived; or, by withdrawing the
veil of appearance, we may uncover its essential reality, and
reveal its truth and beauty. The saint stands at the frontier
of the two worlds. In the midst of the visible world he is a
witness to the invisible—to something which is present in the
deep life of all of us, but which the visible world hides or
reveals according to the way we look at things. It is necessary

that the saints should live among us, that they should be subject, like us, to all the wretchedness of our human condition, and that they should even seem to be overwhelmed by it; for in this way they teach us to be indifferent to all the glory of the world, proving to us in a striking manner that our true good lies elsewhere. The essence of holiness often manifests itself most clearly in the frustration the saint endures, in the pain which is inflicted on him, or which he inflicts on himself, in torture or in martyrdom. In martyrdom certainly, the purity of the witness is most clearly seen. But other types of witness are of a more secret kind. Not all the saints have been called to be martyrs. Yet our imagination needs these great examples as a measure of the distance there is between holiness and success. Holiness is the supreme success in the spiritual order; it is indifferent to worldly success and indeed despises it.

But no one can choose the state of life in which he is placed nor the demands that such a state makes on him. Holiness may be found on the throne, where most men agree it encounters the greatest difficulties. Holiness again may be hidden beneath the rags of a beggar, where indeed one is more often inclined to look for it. But no one knows which requires the greater effort, to resist the demon of pride or the demon of envy. In truth we like to find a sharp contrast between holiness and the state of life in which it exists. Holiness appears most striking when we find it either at the summit of human greatness (when this greatness is forgotten or despised) or when it is seen in the lowest state of human wretchedness (when this wretchedness is accepted and even loved). But it is the mark of holiness to be to the natural eye as invisible as is the world of spirit into which it invites us to enter. The holiness of the beggar or the king is not easy to discover in the features of the beggar or the king; holiness for us is always linked with the wholly interior attitude of mind we assign to it and which finds a mysterious echo in our own souls. And thus our beggar and king resemble the unknown saint with whom we rub shoulders every day without any sign to mark him out for recognition.

The saint may be a scholar, a theologian, or the founder of a Religious Order. But it is not through any of these things that he is a saint. Holiness, it is true, shines forth in all the work he does; even as in the case of king or beggar it shows itself in the way of government of the one or in the outstretched palm of the other. For the saint can be one of the ordinary run of men, who seems absorbed in the most common tasks, at once a solitary and yet accessible to all. His outward life may seem to consist in a mechanical series of habitual acts; yet now and then a familiar yet unexpected gesture on his part is enough to solve, in the most natural way in the world, a hitherto insoluble problem; or a smile, full of radiance and understanding, without in any way altering circumstances, will transform the way in which we look at them. The saint transforms life for us into a perpetual miracle which, without disturbing in any way the natural order of things, shines through that order and reveals itself to us.

4. A POTENTIAL SAINT IN EACH OF US

We must learn to recognize the saints who live beside us and even the saint who is within us, whom we decline to assist in his struggle to be born. The least movement of love is enough to reveal the saint in us and in others, ready to appear. But we do not seem able to give continuity to this first impulse, to give it stability, and to repel the forces that impede its action, the things that form the centre of our interest and our chief point of honour. No saint is immune from such lapses; and none can be sure whether he will be able to pick himself up again, and whether he will be saved or lost. But this is none of our business. Our duty is simply to do our best to keep the saint in us alive. There are in this world only potential saints who come into actual existence by their own effort, through a series of frustrations, trials and failures. It is courage that makes the saint; and courage is no more than confidence in grace that comes from on high and is always available, though we do not always open our hearts to receive it.

The saint seems most often to be a man of strong will who never ceases to strive and to conquer. Yet we may also say that the saint is less strong-willed than most; for the will is always linked with love of self and is always out for victory and for triumph. Now in the saint the will gives way, yielding place to a far more powerful principle of action which, in return for its docility, will raise it to a higher plane: it yields place to love. It suffices that of its own motion the will puts no obstacles in the way of love. And so it happens that our steps towards holiness are always easy and natural, which proves that grace—in the twofold sense we give to the word—is simply the perfection of nature.

We are apt to base our judgements on the laws that rule the world of appearances; this is evident in our immediate circle where others are known to us as they really are and not simply as they outwardly appear. How often we hear people say—or even say ourselves—in the presence of certain souls in whom there is an absence of all self-seeking, and whose bodies seem to share the quality of light and whose deeds are the expression of an ever-active spiritual life: here is a saint. Not that we can ever fathom the secret life of any soul, nor foresee how it may develop. Yet certain contacts we make with others bring us a kind of revelation. In such souls we see the life of holiness in operation and are able to study its formation and its way of expression. We are not obliged to leave this world in which we live; for holiness illuminates it with its own radiance and adds an interior resonance without which it would be no more than a phantom floating in the void.

5. THE FRONTIER OF THE MATERIAL AND THE SPIRITUAL

And yet the saint appears to live in a world apart from our world. It is as though he sees things we do not see, and as though his actions were guided by motives other than the motives that dictate our acts. Sometimes we have the impression that he is beside us, though not with us. And we feel it is so because we see only the surface of reality while the saint penetrates its depth and its true meaning. He makes his home quite naturally on a plane of existence which we can only reach at the price of great concentration and effort. Moreover we cannot dwell for any length of time upon this plane: we have only occasional glimpses of it. For this is a spiritual plane beyond the reach of nature—and one which we rightly call supernatural. Yet the saint belongs naturally there and surprises us with his perfect ease of movement. And by a kind of paradox all the objects we see in the world around us, instead of fading away like mere illusions, now take on the weight and substance they lacked. They become symbols bearing witness to, and integrated with, the hidden values that are revealed to us by the saint, and that find a kind of outward expression in the features of the world we see.

The saint alone has the ability to transcend the dual order of matter and spirit and to combine the two in a perfect unity. And what surprises us most is that in order to achieve this unity he has no need to use the processes of reasoning. No one uses reason less than the saint. The process of abstraction he ignores. He lives on one level with all the aspects of reality. The characteristic effort of our thought is laboriously to search out connexions between the various aspects of things; but the saint is grounded in unity. For him there are not various forms of existence which have afterwards to be brought into harmony, but rather one single centre of energy which produces, almost without knowing it or willing it, these forms that manifest and radiate the activity at the centre. Everything the saint does seems to spring from a source which is outside the processes of intelligence and yet appears to be the most subtle operation of a most lucid and wise intelligence. Every act of his is so akin to ours and so familiar that it seems within the compass of a child. Things seem to respond to his will even before he invites their response. They seem to have no existence beyond the sense-impression by which we become aware of them, and which scarcely differs from the sentiment they stir in our souls. In this way the difference between internal and external, between ourselves and things, is abolished. To the saint the world is not something foreign, nor is it a mystery from which the secret has to be wrung. His dwelling-place is at the heart of the world, in the life of which he always shares; while other men are aware only of its outward appearances without understanding their significance.

This is why the saint is at once the most sensitive and the most spiritual of men: the most sensitive, because nothing in the world finds him indifferent; the most vulnerable also, since it is most easy to reach his feelings and move him to action. He is always in immediate and just relation with persons and things. He is also the most spiritual of men; for every movement of his soul has its origin in an inner initiative which has deep down a rational explanation, though there is no need to formulate it. And so for him freedom and necessity are one: freedom, because he is not determined by any external cause; and necessity, because in no circumstances could he imagine himself acting otherwise.

6. AN UNWAVERING VISION

That which disconcerts us and arouses astonishment mixed with suspicion in some, and admiration touched with awe in others, is that while our lives are beset by the problems of existence, the saint lives among the solutions to these problems. We might rather say that his way of life supplies the solution of all the problems that existence brings. There is always an element of the relative and uncertain in the things that are given or offered to us. But the moment the most transient and apparently insignificant things fall under the hand of a saint they are thrown into striking relief: they are at once what they are and yet something other than they are. Far from the thought of the eternal and the absolute making their wretchedness manifest, they cause eternal and absolute values to appear before our eyes. Far from leading us away from this life towards a dream-world which is always inaccessible, the saint introduces here and now a presence that our nature is always striving to reach; and, instead of disappointing our hope, he fulfils our aspiration. The ambition which lies at the root of metaphysical thinking, to pass beyond visible reality and attain the unseen truth which is its foundation and first principle, has no more than a speculative interest. It can only be fulfilled when it is brought in to act as part of the real order. And this cannot happen save in the life of the saint who animates even his humblest acts with the life of the spirit.

If it is true that the saint always goes to the limits of his powers, that is something we never achieve. But what is the limit of our power, if it be not an absolute sincerity on our part, making all our actions correspond exactly with our thought and feeling, that is, with the deepest and most intimate part of our soul? But for our part we nearly always live on compromise; we are always ready to give way before the opinion of others. The world in which we live and act is a world of make-believe. No one can say that there is any exact correspondence between what it appears to be and what it is. To us it seems that it cannot be otherwise, that outward appearances exist to conceal rather than to reveal our true selves. For us it is a mark not merely of courtesy but even of charity to tone down our feelings, to restrain our natural impulses, and to dress reality in a cloak of artifice, which we think serves to protect everyone and yet deceives no one. The sight of reality in its naked form, so it seems to us, would be too dazzling and too piercing to be borne. Yet the mark of the saint is precisely to fix his eyes on reality with a steady gaze and to compel us likewise to look on it. To us that seems to be beyond the power of men. For the saint the world has no dark side: even what seems darkest he brings into the full light of day. For him appearance and truth are indistinguishable; for truth becomes identified with appearance. To us nothing seems more surprising. The tenuous veil that separated the world of thought from the world of action has vanished. The secret thoughts of the saint take form and life before our eyes. Even his faults are not hidden from us: they are in him a testimony to his human nature. It is only the very ordinary man who conceals his faults, for neither good nor evil has any strength in him. He lacks the courage to pursue either; and by concealing the one he prevents the development of the other. But in the case of the saint the ever-present evil is converted into good; and this revives his spirit and continually spurs him on. It surprises us to find good and evil so close together; but this is because we fail to see how the one feeds on the other and transforms it.

With us ordinary folk there is always a division between what is exterior and what is interior, between truth and opinion, between what we would wish and what we are able to do. The mark of the saint is that he has achieved unity within himself. His life, we think, must be a perpetual sacrifice; because the exterior order of things holds our attention, and we suppose that the interior order must separate us from it; and also because we stand in fear of opinion, since it seems to bring truth into derision; and again because we take refuge in our weakness which, as we judge things, constitutes an insurmountable obstacle to the fulfilment of our most cherished desires. The saint knows no such fear or embarrassment. He always commits his whole self and is therefore never concerned about loss or gain; so he is not conscious of making any sacrifice. How indeed could he sacrifice external things seeing that they are for him no more than interior things in an outward manifestation? How could he sacrifice opinion which is for him no other than truth in an incomplete and still obscure form? How could he sacrifice his own imperfection seeing that he is conscious of an inward power that is constantly making good this same imperfection? He would tell us that by refusing to tread the path of holiness we are sacrificing real goods without which these apparent goods have neither substance nor savour.

7. IGNORING HIMSELF THE SAINT BECOMES ENGROSSED IN EVERYTHING ELSE

But perhaps we ought to say that in holiness the great problem is to discover the precise value we place on self. For self is the principal object of our preoccupations and since it contains them all it is the origin of an egoism in which evil finds a kind of incarnation. It is the hydra with a hundred heads all of which no man has managed to destroy. But there are many who regard the pursuit of holiness, with its concentration on the interior life and on personal salvation, as the most radical and subtle form of egoism. To

SISTERS LIBRARY
ST. JOSEPH'S HOSPITAL
DENVER, COLO.

escape from this egoism we are told to fix our eyes on the world, on the things we can influence, on the persons who constantly seek our help and co-operation.

It would be a great injustice to suppose that the saint is indifferent in these matters. Through his presence alone he succeeds in giving to the things or persons he meets on the way the interior quality they lacked. He does not confine their existence to his own consciousness, nor does he use them as instruments to further his own destiny. He helps them to rediscover their true spiritual home. He reveals to them the source from which he draws and from which all men may draw and which never runs dry. The saint does not offer himself as an example to others, for each of us can find within ourselves the model to which we must conform: the saint merely helps us to find that model.

No one is less preoccupied with the ego than is the saint. It is we who ceaselessly think of our ego either in order to serve it or to subdue it—which is only another way of thinking about it. The mark of the saint is to banish the very thought of it. As a result it is the saint alone who is alive to all that is happening in the world. He is truly alive to himself only so far as he is alive to others and to God. In this way too he transforms our own awareness of ourselves. The ego which turns its attention on itself is bound to meet contradiction in the other ego which is now the object of its attention; and it is driven to deny its existence since this other ego postulates an interior essence which is not its own. But the saint introduces the ego to an interior mode of existence that is indivisibly one in itself and in all the things that are.

It is a matter of wonder to observe that when we empty ourselves of our ego, when we are as it were reduced to nothing, when we are completely denuded of all we have and of all we are, at that moment the whole world enters in to fill the vacant space. And so by a kind of miracle he who enters into himself is conscious of being outside himself; while he who succeeds in going outside himself feels that he is in touch with his innermost being. The saint has no particular desires. He seeks only to be allowed to disappear. He reveals the world to us as God has willed it. He is a saint because he is a permanent witness to the Will which obliges things to reveal their significance to us, and persons to become aware of their vocation. The saint is like a beacon which God has put into the world and which shines all the more brightly the less we see of its centre.

8. OUR CHRISTIAN NAME AND THE INFINITE VARIETY OF THE SAINTS

It is not easy to recognize the differences that exist between saints. There is among them a common character which sets them apart from humanity as we know it; it is a sacred character which makes them the agents of God and enables them to teach us how to discern in each thing the traces of the continuous creation of the world by God. The saints are all equally remote from the world; and yet they show us its true features as though we were looking at it for the first time.

Now it is the saints from whom we derive our Christian name; and this not only reflects their individuality but also brings them close to us in a kind of intimate relationship, so that each of us invokes the protection of one particular saint as though he were the model we should imitate. In our reflection upon names we may well meditate on the echo which is elicited by the name our most familiar friends give us. It is this name which distinguishes us among those of our kinsfolk who bear our family name; and it evokes in each of us the only person who is capable of answering 'I'. The same Christian name, it is true, belongs to many others also, though each one of these is able to answer 'I' in the unique and inaccessible centre of his soul and heart.

In the lives of the saints we meet characters whose originality is so strongly marked that each one differs radically from all the rest, and seems to constitute a separate species even as every angel is said to do. It is therefore easy to see why a particular saint may be a mediator or model for so many men. Each saint represents an ideal type of human being, a privileged type in whom the essence of man comes to share in the perfect essence of God. There is in mankind an infinite possibility; for all the powers of which our humanity is capable must bear witness to their relations with God and be used in a way which will sanctify them. In this way saints come to be; and each one seems to embody one of the potentialities of which we are conscious within ourselves. The saint teaches us how to set these potentialities to work; and in their exercise he is a mediator between God and us. For if all human nature is in some sense embodied in each man, yet the unity of each man has for its centre one of the basic dispositions proper to him. It is a qualitative unity which binds and disciplines all the functions of the soul in one centre or focus of interest and preference. The operations of the soul grow in strength and efficacy when they are employed in the service of an individual vocation that makes demands on them at once exacting and exclusive. It is a grave error to suppose that the unity to which our soul aspires can only be realized under the form of identity. Unity is all the more perfect as it is more diversified. To be one is to be unique and peerless. It is to recognize— and to be content to assume—one's specific individuality.

In the saint one is always conscious at one and the same time of a call which seems to come forth from his very nature, and of an act through which he never fails to respond to that call. All that he does seems to be dictated by what he is, and he appears to be receptive in all things; yet there is nothing that he does not seem by deliberate election to have chosen to do, so that he appears to be creative of what he is. This is the point where in him freedom and necessity, instead of being in opposition, coincide. It is also the point we all aspire to reach. To find out who we are is to find out who we ought to be. The saints show us the way. Each of them acts as a guide, though they teach us to follow our own path rather than theirs. It is the only way in which we can be faithful to their teaching. No life can ever be begun anew, and no existence can ever consist in the mere imitation of another. The rôle of the saints is to show what each of us can make of his own life; and those saints for whom we have a special devotion are like friends with whom we feel a kind of affinity, even though we may not always resemble them; they move our heart and reveal our true selves to us.

The reason why the saints differ so profoundly one from another is that in human nature there is an infinite capacity which no one man can ever exhaust. There is in every man a potential saint who may never come to light. For the same reason new saints will always continue to appear, though none will reproduce the features of those we know. There can be no progress in the order of sanctity, for each saint according to the gifts he has received and the circumstances of his life must always represent what is absolute, unique and inimitable. It is his absolute relation with God that stamps each individual, whatever may be his limitations and his defects, with the seal of the Absolute which makes him a saint.

9. THE SPIRITUALIZATION OF LIFE THROUGH THE MEMORY

We must not fail to recognize that no man seems to merit the name of saint until his life is at an end. This is so in some measure because until the day of his death he is liable to give way to temptation; but it is chiefly because, if the saint is a spiritual being, the past alone can achieve that mysterious transformation of body into spirit which gives significance to our existence in time. This explains how our life is entirely directed towards the future; yet we cannot regard it as fulfilled until it has vanished into the past. The distinguishing feature of the past, as it always seems to us, is simply to destroy that which has already been; so that as we move forward in time we should constantly meet and assume new forms of existence, and never do more than realize, for a fugitive moment before it vanishes, one aspect of life which is gone almost as soon as it appears. We never seem to be rooted in existence, for each instant as it looms up before us is doomed to be recaptured and for ever engulfed in nothingness. The passage between what is to come and what has ceased to be is like birth and death in a simultaneous and uninterrupted series. What we call death brings this strange transformation to a close; and by a single stroke completes the continuous annihilation of ourselves which is the law of all temporal existence. It is as though existence were always attempting to elude the grasp of nothingness and always being defeated.

But this is an illusion. For we only know that the past is the past because we keep the memory of it. Even supposing we were never able to recall the past, it remains a potential memory for us. But what is the significance of memory? It cannot be identified with pure nothingness. Shall we say that its function is to bear witness to an existence we have lost? But memory is in itself another form of existence. The existence we lost was a material and sensible existence, but memory substitutes for it an invisible and spiritual existence which obviously possesses none of the attributes of the former. This may lead us to think we have lost everything, but in fact the new mode of existence has attributes which

the former mode never possessed, and which are by com-
parison with it an unparalleled privilege. For this spiritual
existence is now an existence within us, and even identical
with us. No one can doubt that in memory there is often to
be found a light and a depth which did not belong to the
object at the moment we saw it, nor to the act at the time
we performed it. Memory has detached the event from time
and endowed it with a kind of eternal quality; not that it is
in fact always present to our consciousness, but that we have
the right and power of our own choice to make it re-enter
the stream of consciousness. The memory of an event is
always there at our command, and can be endlessly revived.
It is a new form of existence, intimate, stable and purified,
which can only be thought inferior or of less degree by those
who believe that reality can be grasped only by our hands and
eyes. It was necessary that existence should pass through a
corporal form in order to change into a spiritual type, which
is the goal towards which it tends and which it must finally
reach. We must therefore first die to the body in this world
in order to be reborn in the spirit.

10. THE UNION OF THE LIVING AND THE DEAD
ON THE COMMON PLANE OF MEMORY

But can we agree that holiness has its existence solely in
the subjective kind of immortality which is that of memory?
Here an important distinction must be made. It is in the
memory he has of himself that every human being is able
to spiritualize his own existence and thus obtain a title to
eternal life. Otherwise what could survive of him at the
moment of death? His immortality would no longer be that
of the man who had lived but that of another being entirely
unrelated to him. And however closely we examine the
problem of immortality it cannot be dissociated from the

memory of our past; even the possibility of immortal life can only be justified by the way in which we conceive the relation between our memory and our body, which memory presupposes while detaching itself from it. We can only discover the essence of immortality through the idea of a transformation which memory imposes on events when their substance is annihilated.

But of the spiritual life of another we can never know anything even before his death; and at his death he is no longer anything more than a memory. And one may perhaps suppose that there is a sort of mysterious affinity between the memory we have of him, and the recollection of himself which is all that he now has. Although our senses or our emotions rebel against the idea, we may even be more closely united to the dead than to the living. It is true that we can forget them, and the movement of our lower nature may divert our attention elsewhere. But though we be unaware of it, the dead are close to us and are always ready to respond to our call and to exert on us a far purer and more disinterested influence than that which they exerted in their lifetime.

In this way we are better able to understand our union with the saints. It is an entirely spiritual union through which they enter into our lives and share our deliberations and our designs. Their voices sound in the depth of our souls, awakening there ideas to which it is our duty to attend, and opening out possibilities which it is for us to realize. We live with them in an invisible world—the true world of which all the spirits that exist are members, and which is constituted by their mutual and constant inter-relations. Of this other world our visible world is at once the sign and the instrument; it is therefore only natural that when its work is done it should fade away.

And so we may say that the saints are in our midst even

3

though we fail to recognize them; and yet they only become
saints when their life has run its course, and they are transformed into spirits. It would therefore seem necessary to
make a radical change in the rôle we ordinarily assign to
memory; we are apt to think of it as a sort of substitute for
a reality which has ceased to be there: something which introduces a kind of shadow out of line with what has been,
something to which we have recourse only as a secondary
means of filling the gaps of actual existence. But memory
has a far nobler function; for memory unites in us the temporal and the eternal, and gives an eternal quality to the
things of time, purifying and illuminating them. It is in
memory, as soon as we close our eyes, that we see the significance of every event in our lives and of every action we
have performed. It is memory which enshrines the past in
our soul so that it becomes present to us in a spiritual sense.
Finally it is through memory that our soul enters into itself
and becomes aware of our inner essence; through memory
also, without any effort of will on our part, the saints manifest their holiness and receive the honour which is their due.

II. FROM MEMORY TO THE LIVING IDEA WHICH IS THE SOUL

Here again certain difficulties arise. The saints are individual
beings; yet they seem to infringe the laws that govern individual existence. We would like to know their way of life
and they have passed beyond life. They become saints only
through the memory we have of their temporal existence,
though time has no longer any meaning in their case. We
must recognize too that in the memory we have of them
there is a kind of transfiguration of all the events of their life.
These events now disclose their real significance and take on
the character of types and symbols. The saints themselves

are reduced to their essential being. In the process they lose nothing of what they were before; they do not change into abstractions devoid of life. On the contrary, what is now laid bare is the principle of life within them which was like a flame that had been covered over by cinders till its light was obscured and its vitality paralysed. We are at the point at which memory itself changes into a living idea. All it held that was perishable and that has now perished was only there to enable us to grasp the element of active and significant power. In us this power becomes active when we act, inspiring and sustaining us. It is a medium between God and us. And this living idea is the soul itself which has survived death and rid itself of all the elements of becoming with which it was mixed, and whose sole purpose was to enable it to prove itself and shape its character. How could anything remain of all the wretchedness that time has brought to an end? The living idea present and active within us is a soul with which we are in constant communion. Through this experience alone are we conscious of the relationship which unites souls when they no longer need to use the instrument of the body, which acted as a kind of screen between them. Only those with an undue attachment to earth can imagine that we shall rediscover, even in the life of the spirit, the memories and recollections that are proper to our life on earth, instead of distilling from them the pure essence which, in the happiest moments of our life here below, seems to transport us to another world of sublime and eternal realities.

It is into this other world that the saints invite us to enter. They seem to take us by the hand and lead us towards it. The memories we have of their lives show them still attached to earth, full of weaknesses and subject to every kind of tribulation. Their example gives us a sort of security: our life now seems less precarious and unworthy. The saints help us not merely by their example, but by the strength they give us in times of trial, prevailing on us to turn everything that happens to spiritual uses.

It is easy now to understand why we do not invoke the same saint under all circumstances, and why there should be special saints to whom we naturally turn; since these seem to be more closely akin to us and better able to understand and assist us. We feel from the outset that we are more closely bound to them. Although all men may be endowed with the same powers, they do not all make use of them in the same measure. And as in the case of two friends one supplements and completes what is lacking in the other, so that through their mutual relationship a new being, more perfect than either of them, comes into existence; so in like manner every saint inspires a series of successors who develop and bring into operation all the potentialities he had in him. Through these successors the seed of his example yields a harvest for ever.

The saints show us all we can do and all we can be. They trace back to God the origin of all the possibilities in us. They show us which of these possibilities we are called on to develop and teach us how to put them in practice. Their spirit communicates itself to us. Each of us is able with their help to discover his vocation and fulfil it. This does not imply mere imitation on our part, which might well discourage our initiative; but the saints show us the field where we ought to labour, where our work will prolong their own, though it may not always look very like it. It is through the saints that the material world is joined with the spiritual world and time is merged into eternity. Through the memory we have of them we are able to find a place for them in our hearts; but this same memory has changed them into spiritual beings with whom we are united in the world of the Spirit, where each individual fulfils his unique vocation and is in inseparable communion with all other souls.

12. THE SAINT, THE HERO AND THE SAGE

The saint is often contrasted with the hero and the sage. The saint can be either of these though it does not always so happen. If he is a hero, he is the kind of hero who masks his heroism beneath the outward appearance of submission; and if a sage he often disguises his wisdom under the appearance of folly. Both hero and sage appear to be concerned only with nature, which will and reason seem able to subdue and rule. Our purely human resources suffice to produce heroism and wisdom, but both are far removed from holiness. They do not spring from the same source, nor do they pursue the same end. The hero does not give way to nature: he imposes his will on it, and as soon as a conflict arises he makes his will prevail even if in the effort he succumbs. The sage on the other hand seeks an alliance with nature and makes it serve his ends. He establishes between nature and will a kind of equilibrium, which assures his inner peace and gives free play to his thought and judgement. The hero resists the course of events, even though he be broken in the process. The sage accepts this order and accommodates himself to it, giving it a spiritual significance. Both are concerned only with the values of things. The hero is always prepared to do violence to the course of events so as to force the issue; while the sage falls into line with the course of things in the hope of getting them to bear witness to the values he has at heart. The one is only concerned with conflict, and sometimes even provokes it: the other acts as a peacemaker, and seeks a harmony which he attains at times only by evading conflict. The hero ought only to engage in conflict when the ways of wisdom offer no further help and wisdom itself urges him to take this course. The sage must never decline to take the path of heroism if wisdom can be purchased only at this price. But the hero and the sage are, as we are well aware, men who rely on themselves in their action; they are therefore always in danger of a fall. We are puzzled when we find that one may be a hero in an unworthy cause; and that the sage sometimes sacrifices the better course to a risk that he thinks he ought to take. Heroism has a certain glamour, and that is why there is such a thing as false heroism. Yet heroism may on occasion be unseen and unconscious even on the part of him who plays the hero. The way of wisdom is sometimes no more than an appearance of peace: it is no more than a counterfeit wisdom unless it is the outward sign of inward peace of soul.

Heroism, it seems, is an act and wisdom a state. Acts of heroism always seem to be performed on the impulse of the moment, as if they were implicit in the course of events. Such acts are nearly always followed by a slackening of tension. Few heroes remain on the level of the act which they were once able to accomplish. It is not expected of them. In a life which needs to be continuously renewed and maintained on the level of heroism, an unbroken series of heroic acts is not possible. Wisdom on the other hand seems to belong to time in duration and not merely to the passing moment. The important thing is that it should not falter. We can perform individual acts wisely, but the virtue of wisdom only becomes inscribed in our nature by slow degrees. It is an acquired virtue, and only bears full fruit during the last years of our life.

Holiness is at once an act and a state. It is a state which not merely manifests itself in acts but is in itself an ever-present act, which may occasionally fail of its purpose but is always renewed. And so while heroism belongs to the instant and wisdom to the duration of time, holiness belongs to eternity —but to eternity which is incarnate in time. For this reason holiness always acts in instants of time. It is always accessible, always ready to give and to spend itself in action; yet in its undivided unity it fills the whole of existence and cannot be reduced to one particular instant or even to the totality of all the instants of time. In an instant it opens a way into eternity—into an eternity that lasts and gives its continuum to all duration.

We need not therefore be surprised that the saint often performs actions which appear heroic. But these must not be attributed to heroism if by heroism we mean something that merely implies a fight, and victory in the fight. Instead of going against nature it is in effect through a kind of natural necessity that the saint performs such striking and difficult actions. This is because there is in him a new nature which, instead of being in opposition to the earlier order of nature, spiritualizes it and is at one with it. For all its apparent foolishness his action transcends the wisdom of the most wise. Not that the action of a saint is determined by nice calculations of prudence; but because it is beyond prudence, it finds its inspiration in a higher source, and integrates and transcends all the counsels of wisdom.

13. THE SAINT MAKES OF THE WORLD A PERPETUAL MIRACLE

The mark of holiness is to make us live in an atmosphere of perpetual miracle. We are in that atmosphere when we are conscious of the presence and action of God in all we see and do.

In this respect there is a certain opposition between the action of the scientist and that of the saint. The whole effort of the scientist is to strip the world and life of their miraculous character; yet we know that science fails in its endeavour. For the features of the world as revealed to us by the most advanced science remain as mysterious as—perhaps even more mysterious than—the features that are displayed to our ordinary senses. Yet science seeks to strip the world of every element of miracle because it assumes that the world is self-sufficient, that it consists of a mere concurrence of things or phenomena located in space or time, and linked together by a more or less complex system of laws which are in gradual course of discovery. The spirit of the scientist is thus immanent in the things of the world.

It is none the less a great miracle that there should be a mind capable of apprehending the world as a whole and of learning the science of it. It is for this reason that mind transcends the world. Moreover it is not in this world that it finds its destiny and end. The world serves at once as a means of communication and a place of probation. It must become for the mind or soul not merely an outward show but also a means by which the soul will find its proper fulfilment. It is because the world is an obstacle that it can also be an instrument; and because it rebels against mind it can also be a witness for it. The saint constantly obliges the world to bear witness on the side of the spirit; for he is continually revealing to us the living presence of God in the world. It shines forth even in the least of his words or gestures. The world abounds in miracles, from the tiniest blade of grass to the stars in their courses; from the movement of our little finger to the mighty clash of nations. Yet there is nothing which does not become clear and luminous for one who can find in each thing a sign he is content to recognize and a call to which he is ready to respond.

If we think that the world is nothing more than it outwardly appears to be, it becomes merely a blind and monstrous mass in which we are caught up as in a vice, and which in the end will crush us out of existence. If this were true we might well say that our very existence is absurd. Our intelligence is the judge of all these things, and is therefore outside their jurisdiction. It pertains to intelligence, if existence is within its scope and not beyond its jurisdiction, to take care that the world does not blind its vision nor resist its claims but that it shall become the field of their operation. In this way the world takes on a kind of transparent quality.

It has no meaning except to enable us to measure at each moment the success or failure of our spiritual activity. It need not astonish us that for some minds the world appears to be full of light, while for others it seems to be plunged in darkness. The difference is due not so much to power of intellect as to purity and integrity of will.

It is this miracle at work which the saint continually reveals to us: a miracle in which every thing, while still retaining its own identity, suddenly displays an essence and significance which otherwise would have eluded us. The intelligence is thus restored to its proper sphere of activity. It is not true to say that the saint has turned his back on the world. On the contrary, he is the only one who has access to the deep life of the world, instead of remaining merely on the surface. Far from vanishing like a dream, the world reveals to him the deep foundations on which it rests. For him it reflects the face of God, while for those who look on it through bodily eyes alone it means nothing. To see the world thus transfigured is the privilege of those who, instead of thinking that our natural powers suffice to interpret the world to us, suffer a change of heart which makes them attentive to the presence of God; and from Him proceeds the power to greet all things with the glance of love.

We have endeavoured to analyse the different aspects of this interior conversion by studying in turn the spiritual life of four different saints: St. Francis of Assisi, who showed us so admirably how nature itself is the language in which God speaks to us; St. John of the Cross, who made the painful ascent to the supreme heights of contemplation; St. Teresa, who achieved in practice the perfect union between action and contemplation; and finally St. Francis de Sales, whose aim was to show us that, in the secret depths of each soul, will is inseparable from love.

II

FRANCISCAN SPIRITUALITY

No meditation can be more instructive for one who wishes to understand human nature than the effort to comprehend in a single scheme the unity and diversity of monastic institutions. In such a study the essential characteristics of human nature stand out in strong relief, much more clearly than in the analyses of psychologists or the researches of moralists; for here we find all the powers of the soul ordering themselves in a hierarchy, and being unified by a single act of choice through which each individual soul pledges its whole destiny and defines its true relation with the Absolute.

In the Religious Orders there is one inspiration common to all, though it is manifested in most diverse ways. It is the ardent desire for purity which, we may believe, haunts the depths of the human soul, and urges the most earnest spirits to withdraw from the world; and, by entering into themselves, to live continually in the presence of God. If social life separates us from the divine presence, and if solitude on the other hand helps us to regain it, we can see that the life of the cloister is an organization for spiritual solitude. But this solitude is not a state of isolation which leaves us at the mercy of self-love and all its miseries, for it is only through the divine presence it seeks in solitude that the soul is delivered from its isolation. By submitting to the Rule of a Religious Order, individual souls feel that they are upheld, united, strengthened in the life they have chosen, in which the bonds between man and man, far from being broken, tend always towards what is the model of a true society, namely, a brotherhood. Moreover the life of the cloister would be incomprehensible and even unendurable if it were not at the same time a communion with all mankind, whose fate is always linked with our own. For this communion every human being is responsible according to the measure of his power; and for it, as much as for himself, he must never cease to work, to study, and to pray.

But the very diversity of the Religious Orders is witness to the diversity of powers in all these individual human beings, each of whom has none the less been called to the same spiritual vocation. For humanity in its essence is present in each one of us; otherwise we could neither communicate with nor understand one another. Yet there is as much difference in the character, tastes and gifts as there is in the features of each individual. We are not all appointed to the same tasks; what is required of one human being cannot possibly be fulfilled by another. If each responded humbly and sincerely to the interior summons, and accepted the circumstances in which he is placed, instead of trying to select or alter them, he would immediately cease to compare himself with others; nor would he imitate an activity for which he is not fitted or envy a success he is incapable of achieving.

Even in the order of nature we can distinguish different types of disposition. In the intellectual order we find families or schools of thought. For in this world nothing is abstract; each being has its own irreplaceable originality which always needs to be spiritualized and transfigured, but may never be annihilated. This unique character is apparent in the psychology of the saints, and even among the choirs of angels. The Religious Orders give full scope for its expression; for the spiritual life, always one and undivided, assumes in each particular Order a unique and special character which varies again in each of its members.

If we have chosen Franciscan spirituality for our first study it is because spirituality is here seen in almost its purest form. This is apparent even from the objections so often made against it—that it will have nothing to do with intellectual pursuits; that it holds such pursuits useless, even though the Order has had its scholars and its philosophers. The Franciscan spirit marks a return to a state of simplicity and trust, in which even the struggle against evil is no other than a more direct consciousness of the presence of God, who comes more and more close to us and is more and more active in our lives. In every aspect of the spiritual life we can perhaps find something of the Franciscan spirit, and discern in it, more clearly marked, some of the deepest requirements of the religious life itself.

The message of St. Francis has often been welcomed by the world in general, but for two reasons against which we must be on our guard. The first is for its supposed creation of a Franciscan æsthetic; one might even call it a Franciscan 'manner'. This is shown by the keen attraction so many readers feel for the picturesque element in the *Fioretti*, though one may doubt whether any deep impression is left on their minds other than the sense of certain fresh and delicate images; and again by the transformation of Assisi into a place of pilgrimage where the pilgrim comes to admire the beauty of the scene and to seek in the very light and air a kind of sensuous joy in a spiritual atmosphere that is inaccessible elsewhere. The Franciscan spirit has indeed produced a series of wonderful works of art, but it has always raised art to its own level. All spiritual life perishes if it is reduced to the level of æsthetics.

The second interpretation which tends to distort the teaching of St. Francis is to regard it as nothing more than a gospel of sweetness and gentleness to which the soul surrenders through a mere relaxation of activity, returning thus to a state of childlike innocence. In this state it is humble in the presence of nature and even of animals, and offers no resistance to any obstacles in its way. It accordingly accepts whatever happens as a manifestation of the will of God; and for the struggle against evil it substitutes a habit of non-resistance which is supposed to effect our deliverance—a doctrine which in the last century was preached by Tolstoy, and in our own time by Gandhi. But it is surely a grave error to transform the Franciscan idea into a simple reaffirmation of the primitive goodness of our natural appetites, and a faith in a common fellowship among creatures, which cannot fail to irritate us because it seems insipid or artificial; and even into a negative attitude of resignation and non-resistance, which would always leave God to act, without any obligation on our part to co-operate with Him. This would indeed be to disfigure the Franciscan concept of the human soul, which puts the will at the very centre of our being, where it is always ready to receive and make use of the light and strength that God continually bestows on it. It is this concept that Fr. Gemelli,[1] himself a Franciscan, and many others with him, hold to be the most apt to solve the difficulties and overcome all the anguish of the modern world.

In the holiness of St. Francis everything does indeed seem easy and simple. But we shall wholly fail to understand it if we do not realize that (apart from gestures which are mere external and misleading appearances) the things which are outwardly most simple are those which reveal to us the stark reality behind the veil which hides it from our view. These revelations are most rare and most difficult to attain.

Ozanam calls St. Francis the Orpheus of the Middle Ages. Like Orpheus he tames nature, brings the stones to life, obliges the elements to line up in accordance with the laws of harmony, and brings light to souls that are plunged in

[1] Agostino Gemelli, *Le Message de saint François au Monde Moderne* (Lethielleux).

darkness, transforming indifference into hope and even anger into love. His great achievement was to convert each life, even the most wretched and rebellious, into a hymn of divine praise. It was he who inspired the extraordinary awakening of spirituality which lasted throughout the thirteenth century. St. Louis, the King of France, was a Franciscan; and according to the *Fioretti* he goes to see Brother Giles in the Convent at Perugia. The two brothers fall on their knees in silence in front of each other, but in the divine light their souls become transparent each to the other. St. Francis inspired the paintings of Giotto, who shows us in Umbrian landscapes scenes from the life of St. Francis, where the colours seem to become immaterial, so that only the souls of persons and even things are made to appear. And Giotto, it seems, took counsel with Dante, who mentions him in the Divine Comedy, the theology of which is inspired by St. Thomas, though its Paradise is the Paradise of St. Francis.

What precisely are the reasons for the extraordinary ascendancy which the Poor Man of Assisi exercised on his own age, and which even today reaches out beyond the limits not only of the Church but also of Christendom? They are surely to be found in the state of perfect simplicity, in the complete renunciation of self-love, through which the obstacles separating the soul from God are eliminated, while His presence becomes visible and His action is manifest in all the events of our lives. It shows us in the world a divine order enlightening our intelligence and directing our will if only we be attentive and docile. The conflicts that previously rent our conscience are now miraculously stilled. The very wretchedness of our state, if we embrace that state with love, brings us riches beyond all our desire. Nature which hitherto seemed dark and obscure is now suffused with light; instead of being a hindrance it becomes a minister of grace. Time ceases to divide and is no longer a barrier that makes us yearn for eternity; it brings eternity to us even now. Action is no longer opposed to but even assists contemplation, since it is a way of union with the divine mind and a means of co-operation with the creative will of God. And the renunciation of pleasure, far from depriving us of some good, brings an inestimable reward in the very joy of action and of love.

Let us examine in turn these different aspects of Franciscan spirituality. And first poverty, which in the life of St. Francis and in the Rule of his Order is the cardinal virtue on which all the others depend. The virtue of poverty goes deeper than one might suppose; for it is all one with the interior simplicity through which, in entire confidence, we surrender to God our whole soul, naked and free, devoid of all attachment to anything apart from Him, with a pure and holy simplicity that confounds all the wisdom of the world. Poverty hollows out in our soul a little vacant place which we must continue to enlarge until at length nothing remains but free and empty space for God Himself to fill. The more a soul realizes its wretchedness and insufficiency, the more vividly it becomes conscious of the infinite abundance it needs and seeks, and which even now it begins to receive. The Friars Minor make themselves the least of men. They know that those who humble themselves have the greatest measure of grace, for they create in themselves the conditions which allow God to dwell within them. They desire to be invisible as He is invisible. The sense of His greatness is vouchsafed to them together with the consciousness of their own littleness. The lesson of humility, as the word reminds us, is to keep our feet upon the ground; it saves us from falling yet at the same time it directs our gaze towards heaven. Poverty is the greatest of treasures because it teaches us to renounce all in order to gain all. For true riches consist in not coveting things we lack and in not clinging to the things we have. And he alone who in the sight of God is stripped bare of all else finds himself face to face with God.

Poverty goes still further. It commands us to rid ourselves of all the cares and anxieties which betoken too much regard for ourselves, our feelings and responsibilities and by virtue of which we fail to make to God a full and complete surrender of the care of our destiny. Now it happens that for certain highly sensitive and conscientious souls this sacrifice is the most difficult to make. But God wishes to give us a spiritual ease and purity which will deliver us even from these interior attachments and allow our souls to ascend to Him. For this reason nothing must remain in our souls to weigh them down. Poverty is neither a state imposed on us, nor a gift that is granted to us: it is a deep science we must master. It purifies and frees us from all our former possessions, by revealing their worthlessness; but at the same time it shows us an infinite good which will belong to us if we will consent to belong to it.

As soon as man diverts his gaze from himself he has the whole of nature before his eyes. But is there not in nature an evil principle ever seeking to seduce us, opposing the movement of grace, and detaching us from God, a principle we must resist without ceasing if we are to achieve our spiritual independence? St. Francis judged otherwise. He would admit no opposition between the Creator and His creation. Nature itself is not corrupt; it is our will that corrupts nature. There is in nature an ambivalence which allows room precisely for the exercise of freedom; sometimes we find in it the visible evidence of divine action and are able everywhere to admire its innocence, harmony and beauty; at other times, seeing it in detachment from its Source we can find only the marks of brutality, disorder and sin. Even so, the things nature offers us are forces of which it behoves us to make good use, ideas about God which call for a response, duties which are proposed to us, deep currents in our life the true destination of which we must recognize and which must be rectified and transformed if they deviate from their proper course.

There is no antagonism between God, nature and life because both nature and life proceed from Him and exist in order to manifest and serve Him. The human spirit has no need to struggle against them or to destroy them; it must rather promote them and prove their worth. The universe then becomes a choir offering unceasing prayer to God. For those with true vision the world is always proclaiming the glory of God. St. Francis himself sings the Canticle of the Sun and of creatures. Creatures must be loved, but only as the creatures of God and in the spirit of poverty which forbids love ever to become a desire for possession. Nature now becomes an open road leading to the attainment of our spiritual ends. We can recognize in it the hall-mark of its Author; for faith of its very essence forbids us to discern traces of the Fall without at the same time discovering the signs of the Redemption. In the horror of nature which certain ascetics express there is often much self-seeking and impurity as well as a distrust of life in its simplicity as God has given it to us. Nature must always be for the soul at once a witness and a means of life.

It is therefore unfair to reproach St. Francis for a supposed inclination to naturalism and pantheism. He does not naturalize the spirit: he spiritualizes nature. The same desire which directs us to individual things ought also to detach us from them, by carrying us through and even beyond them towards the Absolute by whom they are maintained in existence, to the centre of light which irradiates them. Then their materiality itself will be seen to dissolve, and only their

4

spiritual significance will remain. They will no longer afford us the pleasure we previously expected, but they will reveal their beauty—an eternal beauty fit only to be an object of contemplation.

One cannot say that this is a doctrine of easy surrender. For which is the more difficult? To anathematize a blind and rebellious nature, or to make it so clear and translucent that it reveals the very features of God? To allow a ceaseless war to be waged between will and desire, or to limit desire to things so simple and pure that the will withdraws opposition and grace perfects the work?

The virtue of poverty and the transfiguration of nature are perhaps the most salient features of the Franciscan spirit. But it would be an error to suppose that such qualities suffice in themselves or that they are founded on a faith in God which dispenses us from the duty of action. Franciscan spirituality is poles apart from Quietism. The Franciscan doctor, Duns Scotus, exalts the will; for how without an effort of will can we practise poverty of spirit and raise up to God all our natural inclinations? The soul which finds its satisfaction in the good things of nature or of fortune looks exclusively to external things and to the sensible satisfaction that they bring. Such a soul is merely a thing among other things: everything that happens to it is due to the influence exerted by objects or events before which it is passive. But the life of the spirit is free; it turns away from external phenomena, for its fate does not depend on them. Its attention is focused on an interior act which it is called on to accomplish, and which constitutes its existence and its very life.

For only through such an act are we able to attain in intention and truth to union with God. It is only in this way that we pledge our whole being. It is a gift of ourselves by which we seem to go beyond ourselves and yet somehow to

re-create our spirit. For he alone can really be said to act
who strips himself of everything and yet despises nothing:
who renounces possession in order through the energy of
love to pass beyond it. But idleness must be banished, for this
leaves us alone with ourselves and invites the devil to enter
in. Poverty commands both work and service. We are too
apt to forget that in Franciscan spirituality knowledge is
subordinated to action; or rather that it strives through action
rather than books to acquire true wisdom. *Tantum scit homo
quantum operatur.* Moreover action and contemplation are
not opposed to one another; at the highest point of the soul
they converge; for contemplation is no more than action
purified and at rest. We must so understand the saying of
St. Bonaventure that action raises us on high: *sursum actio.*

Action can never be purely and simply a means to an end.
It is not directed to an end to which it will be wholly sub-
ordinate. To measure our action we must not be too preoccupied with its success or its failure; for this would be to
imitate those who refrain from sowing lest birds devour the
grain. The supreme worth of action lies in its being an
imitation of God who is Himself Pure Act, and a participation of His will and of His essence; for the very powers that
dispose us to act are given to us by God. By our action we
respond to His call, continuing with our own hands and
without respite the work of creation itself. The holiness
taught by St. Francis is not only, as some suppose, meek, resigned and attentive; it is also resolute, prompt, eager, enter-
prising, indefatigable.

Nor can it be said that action so binds us to our daily
tasks as to make us forgetful of eternity. The truth is just
the opposite. Our act aims at no distant end but seeks only
its proper perfection at the very moment of its doing. Events
as they occur fall one after one into the lap of time, and if

love alone can be said to be truly active, it is through action that we gain an entrance to eternity. The material element of the act is in itself indifferent; and in Chapter VII of the Rule we read: 'Let each one stay in the profession or trade he was following when he was called'. An act can take place only in the present time and is in itself an acknowledgement of our response to what God asks of us.

In this way time and eternity are reconciled. And we admire the lively sense of true psychology shown by St. Francis when he counsels us not only to suit our thought and will to our actual circumstances, but also to cultivate in body and spirit a certain swiftness of movement—a *sancta velocitas*—which will dispose us never to be too soon or too late in our response to His command; never to allow any opportunity for self-love to enter in, and always to be ready to meet any demand that may be made on us. If we follow the course of time and circumstance, not striving to arrest and turn them in the direction of our desires or our dreams, we shall share in the eternal mind of God the vision He has of our temporal life, which He always enlightens and sustains.

The spiritual life causes a plenitude of joy to spring up within the soul; for the soul which desires nothing now possesses all things; and nature, no longer a screen between God and ourselves, reveals the beauty of His creative act; while the act we are called upon to do unites us with the divine act, finding its source in eternity. St. Francis will not allow us to talk too much of the wretchedness of mankind since it makes us unjust towards God; he makes no such sharp separation between God and man as is made by a certain school of Protestant theology (and in an aggravated form by Karl Barth) as if to allow the anguish of our time to find a certain justification. On the contrary, in order to exalt man, St. Francis humanizes God.

But what is the joy St. Francis promises? Perfect freedom in the face of everything which may hold or enslave us, whether it be of the body or of fortune or self-love or even success. Freedom is the exact contrary of revolt, since it signifies whole-hearted consent allied to obedience and love. Freedom also reflects the unity of our interior life, making no distinction between action and contemplation. It is to begin with an acceptance of all that is given to us: acceptance of ourselves and of others. It is distinguished by a spontaneous candour which always goes straight to the point. For a man is what he is in the eyes of God, and no more. This is clear from the example of Brother Giles: 'In his acts and in his words he desires to be seen and known just as he is and in the utter simplicity in which God has created him'. And here is the counsel of perfection: 'Seek nothing but what the Lord shall give you. Love others just as they are'. And so we learn never to ask our neighbour to do more than we can do ourselves; to bear with him even as we would have him bear with us if we were in his place; not to boast more of the good that God has done through us than of what He has done through others; always to be gracious, amiable, good-humoured to all, so that our presence may not fail to sustain and help them.

Joy is akin to fortitude in readiness and resource. Conformity with the will of God implies patience and resignation in face of every insult and every misfortune; for these things do not excuse us from working and praising God. On the contrary (according to Paragraph 10 of the Rule), the spirit of joy fills each one with the desire to be such as the Lord would have him be, whether in sickness or in health; lovingly enduring suffering with pure and perfect resignation; and never forgetting that even in heaven every soul is in some kind of relation with all other souls in purgatory or in hell. In this way perfect joy compensates for all the sufferings of mankind, enduring and accepting them, since it transcends and transfigures them all.

There are certain laws in the spiritual world: 'If you love, you will be loved. If you fear, you will be feared. If you serve, you will be served.' But the spirit of true joy transcends these rules. 'For he alone is truly happy who loves and does not desire to be loved, who serves and does not desire to be served, who does good to others and yet does not wish others to do good to him.' Joy in this way becomes identical with peace, as is clear from the well-known saying in the Testament: 'God revealed to me the words of our salutation: "The Lord give thee His peace".' It was joy that reconciled in the soul of St. Francis the most opposite powers; for joy made him at once the most independent and yet the most submissive of souls, one in whom a disciplined calm co-existed with demonstrations of deep feeling, and who was able to combine an active will with complete abandonment to the will of God, and to unite a naïve simplicity with downright daring in the supernatural order.

Henri Bremond liked to bring together prayer and poetry, which was indeed in the Franciscan spirit. For it is proper to poetry and to prayer to make nature translucent with supernatural light. St. Francis was the 'troubadour of God'. He lived continually in His presence. In his prayer there was never a lament, scarcely even a petition. As soon as his soul was raised to God it sang a canticle of thanksgiving. But none of the gifts he received ever obscured for him the evil from which he sought to be rid. Penance was the only reward he looked for in prayer.

St. Francis never thought, as some have supposed, that all purely human sentiments could be so mortified that the soul would finally experience nothing save the delight of uninterrupted union with God. The life of the spirit here below cannot be lived without effort, without affliction, without even a taste of bitterness. The real difficulty lies in learning to accept and use these trials as a firmer and surer means of coming close to God. The true Franciscan ideal is austere and strenuous. One may see it in the description a Friar Minor gives of the ties which still bind him to earth: 'To love and not wish to love, to desire and not wish to desire, to be thrilled by the beauty of this passing life without desiring to enjoy it, to let oneself be carried away by the current and yet go against it, to be stirred by the fever of high achievement and yet remain steadfast at the sentry-post'. At the very centre of the spiritual life there is sometimes a secret affliction which must be borne with unfaltering will. Fr. Gemelli thus describes a Franciscan friar: 'He lavished on others consolations which Providence denied to him. He learnt the secret of understanding them through his own hidden cross, his inability to feel that God loved him, his habit of loving God without any consolation, and the constant lack of either a friend or confessor who understood him.' How great must have been the desolation of such a soul who was yet destined by God to bestow on others the very peace which was denied to him.

Where then is that naïve and appealing optimism sometimes attributed to St. Francis? The distinguishing feature of his message is its unique affirmation of the value of the life and existence we receive from the hands of God. Here God is no longer hidden behind the world, and the Creator is not exalted by denouncing His creatures. For one whose heart is aflame with love the world appears to be the very countenance of God. Every good thing given to us comes from Him. Poverty, suffering and death come to life as Lady Poverty, Our Sister Suffering and Our Sister Death. If we look on them as the ambassadors of God we can acknowledge the good gifts they bring us. St. Francis had the power of revealing the hidden goodness in every thing and every event. It was said of him that 'he brought every creature, the gentlest and the most cruel, and even inanimate things, into one brotherhood. He looked upon them all with so pure and tender a glance that they seemed to share in the redemption of the world.'

It is difficult to bring to unity all the distinctive features of the Franciscan spirit. Yet what strikes us above all is its perfect simplicity that neither self-love nor the discourse of reason nor any kind of effort can ever divide. It is a combination of purity and ardour—a natural spontaneity developed and illumined by grace. The soul of St. Francis was so unified in God that all the conflicts which rend the consciences of others were stilled in him. Everything which for ordinary men is an obstacle to be overcome only through a struggle which exhausts their strength was somehow transmuted by him at a glance; he changed it into a force which seemed to be lent him to bring him still closer to God and which stirred him to fresh acts of thanksgiving. 'The Good to which I aspire is so great', he says, 'that all my suffering is turned into joy.'

But he had not been able all at once to reach this state of spiritual renunciation which did away with all power of preference and obliged him to welcome, cherish and love whatever came his way in a world in which everything reveals the will of God and bears the mark of His presence. Let us recall what he says in his Testament: 'While I was yet a prey to sin the sight of lepers filled me with loathing. Then our Lord Himself led me among them and I had compassion on them. And when I left them what had formerly seemed loathsome was filled with spiritual and even physical sweetness.' What always surprises us in St. Francis is that he is so completely human; he so fully understands our frailties; he utters no curse and no condemnation. He reflects at once the spontaneous movements of our human sensibility, all the aversions of our heart and of our flesh, which are little by little transmuted into tenderness and to an active sympathy with our most secret infirmities. He gives us a solution of the problem of evil, not by denying its existence (as a certain naïve optimism that is sometimes attributed to him might have done), and not by contending against it like St. George with the dragon. He confronted evil with the love which enabled him to lay hold of the evil that was in his inmost heart; and in this way he turned and led it back to the source where all life is nourished even as he did with the savage wolf of Gubbio.

It would therefore be a grave mistake to interpret the simplicity of St. Francis as a kind of return to primitive nature to which we need only surrender ourselves for Paradise to reign upon earth. The simplicity that makes our actions so easy can only be reached after a severe process of purification. The goal of this Franciscan simplicity is not nature: nature at least is not its end. But it sees in nature the intention of the Creator, the call He makes to us and the offer of His outstretched hand. The simplicity of St. Francis meets life with such confidence, ardour and joy that it is ready to accept all hazards because it is certain that with the help of God it will overcome all difficulties and turn all things to good. Such simplicity does not reject nor exclude any of God's gifts; what it does reject is that kind of attachment which turns them into objects of possession. It requires us to accept them only as gifts so that through them our love shall go exclusively to the Giver of all gifts.

Here then is the solution of the traditional conflict in the history of the spiritual life between nature, where evil seems to rule and turn us away from God, and the inner impulse which carries us towards Him while compelling us to struggle against all the forces which are at work in the world. This view of the world has caused many thinkers to propound the theory of a dual order in which good and evil are perpetually at war. Even in our own time we find in various works of Christian apologetic the idea that nature is evil, that it is the work not of God but (as Plato held) of an imperfect demiurge or of a powerful demon whose evil-doing is perpetually being put right by God. The work of God the Redeemer, we are told, precludes belief in God the Creator. Such theories point to a state of mind and conscience, which, having failed to fashion unity within itself, projects its own interior conflict into the ontological order. St. Francis found an entirely different solution; but this solution is not a truth to be viewed objectively; it is rather a truth which only comes into existence for such generous souls as are able to turn it into a living principle in their experience and practice. Nature is only evil if it is separated from God: in that case it may even turn against Him. But if we look on nature with understanding and love it becomes a medium between God and us, the ladder by which God's action descends on us and by which our souls ascend to Him.

The part played by asceticism in the development of Franciscan spirituality is too often overlooked; to some it has even seemed to be a sort of betrayal of the true Franciscan spirit. The truth is that Franciscan asceticism here assumes a very subtle form and is no longer limited to the voluntary discipline to which it is too often reduced. We may well ask ourselves which is the harder task: to offer a blind resistance to all the impulses of our nature, or to suffuse them with light, spiritualize them, strip them of the self-love which disfigures them, and discover in them forces that come from a higher source and can always be transformed and sanctified?

It may be helpful to bear in mind the image of St. Francis

as he really was. This will prevent us from identifying spiritual with natural simplicity. We know that he not only spoke the French language but that he preferred to use it in moments of emotion or enthusiasm. He read romances of chivalry. And all the sentiments he aroused in the depths of the human soul were not mere impulses of nature but were refined and pure sentiments that are too often darkened and dominated by the flesh, though they always retain their original force and appeal, and the body ought in turn to accept their rule and loyally serve their ideal. This was the 'courtly love' which Dante felt for Beatrice in her lifetime and which led him to find her in Paradise; where she is identified with Theology and unfolds truths hidden from mortal eyes which the perfection of love is alone able to reveal.

St. Francis never, as is sometimes thought, adopted the unconventional standpoint of recommending us to break with all the obligations of everyday life. No one more than he infused the fullness of the spiritual life into all the humble and insignificant acts in the round of everyday existence to which men pay scant attention or from which as from an irksome bondage they seek to be delivered. But the intention behind all these humble actions can give them an equal value with the noblest deeds. For God is in their doing and His light shines in them. He never asks us to change our outward way of living. Even when a man starts to reform his life he must still fulfil his daily tasks without desiring to be relieved of them. But reality for him now lies in the invisible world; it even shines through all the movements of corporal life and colours all he sees and does. Once he has discovered this reality within, it fills the whole world and radiates from everything around him. Visible and invisible now become one. And everywhere the opposition between them which formerly caused uneasiness and tension in the soul comes to an end, leaving the spirit in steady equilibrium and with a more active and vital unity.

Take for example solitude, the only sure refuge where the soul can find God. St. Francis never ceased to seek out solitude and to commend it. It was in search of solitude on Mount Alvernia that he received the stigmata; and his state of interior recollection was so profound that no external call could ever disturb his peace. But his state of solitude was removed from all egoism and complacency; and far from saying that he abandoned solitude it would be truer to say that when he turned his glance inward he opened the window of his solitude on the world. Everything he met upon the way, whether bird or plant or other creature, seemed to find a place in his solitude without interrupting it. No man ever bestowed more freely on others his entire attention and the gift of his whole self; for these were an analogy of the presence and of the gift God makes of Himself at all times and to all creatures. The brethren of St. Francis were united in a twofold brotherhood, among themselves and with their fellow-men; each one was so united with all the rest that he became to them as transparent as he was before God.

It has often been said that St. Francis had a contempt for letters and that he viewed with indifference and even with distrust all the science and learning that man can acquire. It is a fact that he did not seek truth in books, because like Descartes he had before his eyes the great book of creation. He did not indeed learn in created things the same lesson as Descartes; for he needed neither elaborate reasoning nor subtle analysis. He saw the light of truth with amazing swiftness, and for him to see the truth was at once to act upon it. Moreover can one say that his Order rejected science seeing that it produced St. Bonaventure, Scotus, Ockham, Raymond Lull and Roger Bacon? We might say that these scholars never followed learning for its own sake; but only to make their way through the realm of knowledge as they made their way through the realm of nature—using it, as it were, and yet not using it, and finding in it what they found in the wonders of nature, yet another way of praising God. 'Woe to learning', said Bossuet, 'which does not turn to love.'

There has perhaps never been a more receptive soul than St. Francis. Of all men he had the most spontaneous and delicate sensitiveness and was deeply moved by all his contacts with nature, with his fellow-men or with God. His soul was always open to fresh inspirations. One may say it had no secrets or again that it was the secret of Everyman made known to all men. His mere existence in the world was enough to reveal to each man the presence of a hidden treasure, an active faith that was also a creative force. The spirituality of St. Francis is imperious in its demand; it asks nothing less than that we should attain to perfect joy—the true sign of our union with God. And it insists that we attain this joy in spite of all the trials we have to endure and that are a constant affliction to our self-love. Such joy means freedom regained; it is a hospitality of heart and mind, which never refuses any offer or request. It implies unshakeable trust united to the infinite power of love.

But it may be asked: can the will alone suffice to awaken love in a soul which is cold or barren? Certainly this could not happen unless there were identity between the love that God has for us and the act by which He calls us into existence. Our love for God is worth nothing unless we see in it the very love by which God loves Himself in us. The thought is awe-inspiring, for we cannot fail to ask ourselves if we are worthy of such a love. The spiritual life according to St. Francis is a kind of perpetual miracle; those who ignore it live in a world in which cause and effect are linked in a rigid and mechanical manner, and where the interplay of desires compels us ceaselessly to pursue particular ends in the lack of which we are unhappy and in the attainment of which we find disillusion. The truth is that this world is a symbol or witness to a world beyond. Its meaning is revealed only to the pure of heart. At all times and under all circumstances it points the way to God, and teaches us how to conform to His will and be re-united to it. At the moment of death the soul of the saint is scarcely conscious of release: for already in this life he has known deliverance.

III

ST. JOHN OF THE CROSS AND
CONTEMPLATION

THE diversity of the Religious Orders admirably portrays the diversity of those interior movements through which the soul strives for union with God. It is the mystery of our human destiny that we are at once so alike and yet so unlike each other; that we should all be called to the same end and yet attain it in such manifold ways. But there is infinity in the depths of the human soul; and each one of us, by discovering his own powers, and developing his own gifts, draws on this infinity and expresses it in his own fashion. When we follow most faithfully our personal vocation, and are most true to ourselves, when we respond to the plan God has for us, we lose the sense of solitude and isolation, and realize through our fellowship with others that we have been given a special task; and however humble this task may be, we alone are able to fulfil it. Philosophers are apt to use the terms individual and universal as though they were mutually exclusive, but the terms are inseparable; for if we were to relinquish what is individual in us, our lives would become artificial, abstract, anonymous; while if we directed everything to our individual service, we should confine the universe within the narrow limits of our ego, where it would go on narrowing until in the end it vanished.

Now the first thing we notice in the Monastic Orders is that their members separate themselves from the world, which need be no more than a severance of all the ties that bind us to it, and a rejection of all the allurements that beguile us. But such a separation has value only because it prepares us for, and indeed already produces, a more perfect spiritual communion with all the rest of mankind, towards whom in future we undertake a certain responsibility in all our thoughts, acts and desires. Again, by choosing solitude with all its exacting demands, the individual recognizes the particular destiny to which he has been called by God, who wills him to consecrate to it his whole being and his life and all the resources at his command. In this way the diversity of the Religious Orders reflects the diversity of the powers of the human soul. Each several Order offers to the soul a privileged mode of action which subordinates but does not suppress the other powers of the soul. The soul, while remaining true to its particular end, must always go beyond it and transform even the humblest task in an active and constant awareness of God.

It was this awareness of God that filled the life of St. Francis of Assisi. He achieved such a miracle of renunciation that he was able to find even in extreme poverty an abundance of riches. He had freed himself from all attachment to the good things of the world and the flesh; and in renouncing all these things, he destroyed at the same time all the barriers separating him from the creative act, the source of infinite bounty that is always available to us. As each thing was taken from him, his horizon became enlarged. Every material loss was changed into a spiritual gain. Humility, which began by being no more than complete renunciation of possessions, became pure love; and in the giving of itself was constantly enriched with new gifts. The work of creation continued to unfold itself before his eyes. Spiritual force penetrated and transfigured his daily life. His slightest gesture became dematerialized and revealed only the pure intent that animated it. Any contact with another human being seemed to restore to that being his original simplicity, to take away from him the cares and burdens of the flesh, to release him from his chains and to oblige him to rediscover in the depths of his soul the original impulse—too soon forgotten—by which God gave him movement and life. Nature ceased to be indifferent or hostile: every living thing—even the inanimate world—bore witness to the Creator and His creative act, and became a means given by God of entering into communion with Him, revealing through its natural beauty the spiritual light which our human eyes are incapable of beholding.

There is a particularly close affinity between the spirit of St. Francis and the spirit of Carmel; yet neither in their thought nor in their aspirations do they follow the same path. In both we find a great gift of poetry, as if the spiritual life found in poetry its most moving and delicate manifestation. In both again we find the same renunciation of all possessions; a renunciation which destroys the limits of our finite existence and brings Infinite Being within our grasp.

But there is a wide difference between the poetry of the Poor Man of Assisi and that of St. John of the Cross. The poetry of St. Francis praises God continually for having revealed His presence through His creatures. It extends to the whole panorama of nature. And even in the inner life of the saint it reveals a spirit so spontaneous and innocent that it purifies everything it touches, transfiguring the ugliness of the world, freeing everything from the fetters of the senses; and, by showing us the relation of each thing to God, making it translucent with supernatural light.

The poetry of St. John of the Cross is quite different. It is not inspired by the trivial events of daily life nor by the pageantry of nature. It gives utterance to a mystical theology which sounds like the commentary on a canticle issuing from the uttermost depths of the soul, announcing its most intimate and secret aspirations, and utilizing sense-images only as symbols designed to interpret and convey their meaning.

It is no longer nature which, in spiritualizing itself, reveals to us the goodness of the Creator. It is now the soul which, descending into the depths of its own essential being, enters there into direct relation with God, having no need to seek and contemplate Him through the works of His creation. Nature is no longer linked with the divine life, though it may inspire thoughts which interpret that life to us.

Similar differences appear in regard to renunciation. The poverty of St. Francis stripped him of the good things of the flesh and of all the desires that link us to these things. The world revealed itself to him in a flash as God intended it to be: the clouds of darkness rolled away, suffering was relieved and cruelty subdued. In such a world human passions find no place, for they are transfigured with light and take on new meaning. The veil which obscured the truth of things and showed a world of blind and unhappy creatures separated from each other and from God, and always at war with one another, is set swiftly aside. The true order of things is now revealed and exhibits a harmony between our will and our deepest desire; while this desire in turn corresponds with grace freely offered and accepted. It is enough that we cease to covet natural goods for them to be restored to us, but so transmuted that they retain only the spiritual essence of which they were at once the shadow and the promise.

With St. John of the Cross renunciation assumes an altogether different aspect. Here nature appears to be forgotten. The created world no longer occupies our attention. The problem is not to repel its attractions nor to withstand the temptation to possess it; nor to see it as it is, that is, as an admirable witness to divine action moving us to a constant prayer of praise and thanksgiving. Our action is no longer of the simple and spontaneous kind that adds nothing to nature, though it assumes its form, and differs from it not in appearance but only in origin. The relation between the soul and God is no longer effected through the works of creation. The visible world no longer counts. The soul is aware only of itself, of its constituent powers and of the conditions of their exercise. It purifies these powers, and directs them away from the world, instead of teaching them to see the face of God in created things. It detaches them from all the particular objects that used to minister to their satisfaction. For these it has no use save as a pure means of mounting to their Source, without the soul being corrupted or lost in the sensible satisfaction of an intermediate end. Renunciation is for St. John of the Cross a total rejection of all the material or spiritual goods that one can describe or possess. It leaves only the Pure Act which created these things. We no longer have to transform the world in which we live in order to perceive the spiritual reality it reveals to the pure of heart. Our concern now is to turn our thoughts so as to find in God Himself—and not as He appears in His handiwork—the supreme object of contemplation, and so give all the powers of the soul their proper and most powerful and efficacious mode of action.

Such is the secret of the *Dark Night* into which the soul begins to enter once it has renounced all the knowledge it seemed to possess, all the desires that allured it, and all the things to which it gave preference or in which it found content. The *Dark Night* is a going-out from oneself, a process of purification. One is often tempted to reproach the mystics not only for the language they use—which describes the movements of the soul rather than the reality of things—but also for a lack of spiritual resolution they seem to show, where intellect and will apparently cease to function. But we must not in this matter allow ourselves to be misled. The *Dark Night* is not without its relation to the universal doubt which induced Descartes, the most lucid and independent of thinkers, to reject everything that was already the object of his belief or attachment, but which had only an individual and subjective significance. In this way he elicits the pure thought that affirms nothing unless it be of certain knowledge, and which to begin with credits itself with nothing though it is capable of assimilating all truth. And here we recognize an intellectual ambition which would be without precedent if it were the achievement of an individual mind acting alone; that is, if Descartes did not discover in his own thought a participation in the divine thought which enlightened and upheld him, and gave him at all times confirmation and assurance, even in the presence of truths that seemed self-evident. Here one can see at least that the human soul always moves to the same measure: it cannot share in Truth and Goodness until it is purged from error and evil; it must break all the bonds that unite it to the finite before it can discover the infinite; it must detach itself from appearances to apprehend reality, and forget self if it is to find God.

We are not seeking to identify the initial movement of the thought of Descartes with that of St. John of the Cross. In the Cartesian doubt, renunciation is no more than a preliminary operation which is soon transformed into a habit of acquisition, while in the *Dark Night* it is because the soul goes forth from itself that it suddenly becomes conscious of fulfilment. To be fair we must recognize that for Descartes truth, although depending upon an activity of the spirit, is none the less received as a kind of revelation; whereas for St. John of the Cross nothing can be given unless the soul first desires and consents to it. But whatever may be the extent of this reservation, one cannot deny that in Descartes there is in the first place a certain self-assurance, based it is true on confidence in God who is its source; while in St. John of the Cross confidence in God no longer implies

confidence in oneself, and indeed comes into existence only
when confidence in oneself has come to an end. Humility,
of its inherent power, now suffices to bring us the presence
of God, without any need on our part for further effort to
attain it. Indeed it would seem as though all the reflection
in which our mind engages acts merely as a screen to hide
God from us. The act of humility by which we turn away
from all our possessions in order that the presence of the
supreme reality may be afforded to us is not an act of the
intelligence which would select the successive steps to be
followed; it is an act of love, the only act which, by detaching
the soul from itself, is able to unite it with the Supreme
Being who is the goal of its desire. Here intelligence is the
fruit of love. By a kind of paradox, as long as we continue
to be preoccupied with ourselves we are drawn with in-
satiable curiosity towards exterior things. When such curiosity
ceases, interior recollection reveals a power of pure love
which detaches us from ourselves and from external things.
The effect of perfect renunciation is to eliminate every inclination and every movement towards an intermediate end.
'To love is henceforth our whole activity.' It animates all
we do.

The same paradox is to be found in our relation with God;
for it is when we adore Him as a Hidden God that we are
most closely united to Him. Thus, positive theology does not
eliminate negative theology; it is at once its fulfilment and
reward. The *Dark Night* merely puts into practice the words
of St. Paul: 'Eye hath not seen nor ear heard, neither hath
it entered into the heart of man, what things God hath prepared for them that love Him' (1 Cor. ii. 9). It is easy now
to understand the solemn and lovely formulæ of St. John
of the Cross which have often been misunderstood and
regarded with suspicion because they are so radical and
intransigent: 'To relish everything, to know everything, to

possess everything, to be everything, one must desire nothing, relish nothing, know nothing, possess nothing, be nothing'. The spiritual life allows no room for compromise: in practice we stumble and fall, but the choice we make is unconditional. It cannot develop nor even exist save in a soul which aims at absolute perfection. Hence those simple and moving similes through which St. John of the Cross shows us that where the whole man is committed there can be no question of 'more' or 'less'; for the most trifling things that detain his attention are enough to distract and destroy him. 'It is the same thing if a bird be held by a slender cord or a stout one; for both equally prevent it from flying away. It is true that the slender one is the easier to break; still, easy though it be, the bird cannot fly away unless it severs the cord completely.' And again: 'When a vessel is full of liquid, the slightest crack— unless it be repaired—is enough to empty it to the last drop'.

By a remarkable coincidence, the *Dark Night* elicits the successive stages of the Cartesian doubt, which first rejects all knowledge received by way of the senses; and next all knowledge acquired by way of intellect, as a prelude to the discovery of its true nature by the thinking self. And so in magnificent yet mysterious poetry, the *Dark Night* elaborates its three successive phases; first, the twilight in which we reject all the objects of sense; then the deep darkness in which we get rid of all the furniture of the mind; and finally the dawn in which the divine light begins to appear. But this dark night does not signify a state of torpor or sleep of the powers of the interior life. It is an active night, due to an effort of the will, and having a twofold effect, namely, a severing of all particular attachments and a return to the creative source by which our spiritual life is ever being renewed. The secret of St. John of the Cross is to create in the soul an activity so entirely free and pure, that it is troubled by no reservation that might otherwise hinder its movement,

by no prepossession that might distract its unity, by no
desire that might come to dominate it. He who desires to
make the ascent of Mount Carmel, St. John of the Cross
tells us, must carry no burden which will weigh him down.
And with admirable simplicity he gives us a maxim which
might well serve as a universal rule of conduct: 'The more
the soul advances in interior perfection the more the operations of its powers cease in regard to particular objects. It is
now able to comprehend all these objects in one pure and
all-embracing act.'

We must not suppose, however, that in the unity of the
act of contemplation there is an abrupt cessation in the
exercise of the powers of the soul. The nothingness into
which the *Dark Night* leads us removes only the boundaries
which limit the individual powers of the soul, when they
exalt the object they seek or the end they pursue above the
spiritual energy from which they proceed, and of which
their several acts are no more than the evidence or the expression. Contemplation only seems to eliminate the operations
of our spirit because it transcends them. In fact, it implies
and includes them. By removing the boundaries which limit
these operations contemplation restores to them the infinite
energy that each of our actions subdivides. Contemplation
unites all the powers which had hitherto been in opposition;
it first plays a minor rôle in merely removing boundaries but
later is cast for a major rôle whereby we regain the whole
momentum of spiritual energy that these obstacles checked
and interrupted.

Nowhere do we find passages of greater depth or beauty
than in the Third Part of the *Ascent of Mount Carmel* where
St. John of the Cross explains how the faculties of the soul
may be purged and spiritualized. We are here at the juncture
of soul and spirit, or if you will, of the psychological and the

supernatural orders. We see most clearly how our two lives of nature and of grace do not oppose and contradict but mutually condition and supplement each other. We are able also to understand the different functions and operations of the soul; these we can employ, to be sure, in a purely human way, but they only reach their full signification when they elicit and make possible a purely spiritual form of action which they prefigure, though it transcends them. The primary function of our body is to manifest our individual existence and then to allow the exercise of our freedom, which takes existence for its matter and gives it a new form.

Consider the faculties which operate within us: understanding, which gives us knowledge of things; memory, which restores their image to us; and will, which always proposes some end to be attained. But let the understanding purify itself, let it cease to entertain any particular and determinate images, let it empty out all the ideas which formerly held its interest; or again let it turn to the principle which enables us to seize each thing in its representative idea —nothing then remains in the understanding but a centre of light which illumines everything we can know in this world without being itself an object of knowledge. The act of understanding is thus transformed into an act of faith.

Now let memory in turn purify itself of all the images which filled it, allowing its recollections to run freely, without adhering to any of them in day-dream or reflection; let it reach a state of spiritual detachment which banishes all preoccupation, and all attachment to things which were in the past the objects of its predilection; in the emptiness that memory thus creates within the soul, it is rid of the burden of the past, and the future opens out before it. But memory makes no effort to determine, that is to say, to delimit the future. It goes out to meet the future, waiting upon it in a spirit of hope and confidence, untarnished by any desire that springs from self-love. The act of memory is thus changed into an act of hope. And the more memory denudes itself, the greater will be its hope.

Next let the will in its turn follow the same path, no longer seeking dominion or conquest, without preference for this end rather than that other. Let it turn back to its own origin— that is to say, to the generosity of that creative act which refuses to serve individual egoism, or to be captivated by any privileged and exclusive object, keeping before it the vision of the One Reality who is its animating impulse and the only end worthy of its devotion. The act of will is thus transformed into an act of charity.

We see now that the faculties of the soul must cease to be busied with the things of the world if they are to be used aright, and that they must be emptied of all created things in order to be filled with God. It is when they are exercised without the use of shapes and images that they bring us to God who is Himself without shape. Instead of losing contact in this way with the habitual objects of their thought, the value and meaning of these objects seems to be enhanced. The operations of the understanding reach the fullness of their illumination only in the light of faith. The images that fill our memory become a source of revelation only if we see in them the promise of hope. The resolutions of our will have strength and firmness only if they are inspired by an ardent charity.

Like Descartes again, St. John of the Cross will not allow us to despise the passions of joy and sorrow, hope and fear, since they are powers of the soul that we must always control and re-direct to God. He tells us that the night of sense should be considered less as a release than as a reformation and restraint of the passions; and the reason, he adds, is that the disorders of our animal nature have their roots not in the body, but on the contrary, in the spirit. The passions, moreover, do not come into play separately. They are always linked and interdependent. 'The wings of each one of these passions are joined to those of each of the others so that in whichever direction the soul turns—that is, in its operation—the others go with it at least virtually also. When one of them descends, they must all descend, and when one is lifted up to heaven, they will all be lifted up.'[1] Joy exceeds all the other passions and brings into exercise all the faculties of the soul instead of, as has been thought, destroying their cohesion and their utility; in this way it represents the perfection of both thought and will. And we may well weigh each word of the definition of joy as 'an affection of the will for those things it considers desirable; where the soul apprehends the cause of its satisfaction and is free to enjoy it or not'. How far we are from the emotional romanticism, to which false mysticism inclines, that seeks states of pure sensibility in which the soul finds pleasure in its own internal activity and so dispenses itself from the duty of external action. The criterion of spiritual joy we are given is precise as well as exacting. We are told to rejoice in all the goods bestowed on us, yet without any sentiment of possessiveness or of ownership. He who finds in these things a personal and individual good misses the true sense of joy and contentment. Every movement of joy that is not directed to the glory of the Creator is lacking in purity; we must subdue it rather than surrender to it; for true joy requires that the heart be free to go to God. Only he who refuses to allow created things to fill his heart is master of them. If created things capture his will, he does not possess them: they possess him.

In St. John of the Cross, as in all the contemplatives, we are surprised to find (in spite of their supposed inclination to the contrary) that they have a developed sense of measure

[1] Cf. Ezechiel i. 5–12 (Douay): Ezechiel's vision of four beasts with one body which had four faces, the wings of the one joined to those of the other. St. John of the Cross says: 'This figure denotes the will with its four passions'. (Tr.)

and proportion. One finds also a regular conformity with the requirements of reason, which they are supposed to despise; a positiveness of a concrete and continuous kind, a close and constant contact with the truest and deepest experiences of daily life. We observe the same characteristics in the life and works of St. Teresa, not indeed without some surprise, as though we expected that the perfect union of the soul with God would tend to destroy rather than to produce such characteristics. But should not this constant return to the creative source of all our activities endow them with poise, strength and illumination? Why should it deflect our activity away from reality instead of enabling it to penetrate and invest reality with order, harmony and direction—the very marks of the spirit once it begins to operate? The contemplative life of St. Teresa was in no sense opposed to her active life; for it was in the active life that she expressed and proved and realized herself. She mastered even the most powerful wills without herself having to make any effort of will; such decision, despatch, moderation, balance, energy and achievement bore witness to a supernatural presence which never failed to give her light and strength. Only a state of uninterrupted contemplation could have endowed her with these qualities.

Now turn to St. John of the Cross. Not only does this great mystic proceed according to the Cartesian method, which looks only to reason for its justification; but he will not allow contemplation to dispense us from any of our duties. Contemplation should rather teach us to recognize these duties and fulfil them more perfectly. And he warns us that 'on the day of judgement God will punish the sins of many souls whom He has illuminated and enriched with virtues and other gifts; because such souls, relying on the converse they had with Him, failed in many respects to fulfil their duties'.

The most striking feature in the writings of the Saint is, on the one hand, his refusal to hold back anything, the almost reckless daring of his renunciation of self, which commits him at every turn to an absolute obligation; and on the other hand, the extreme prudence which makes him fear the pursuit of all the extraordinary ways in which souls seek to be more perfectly united to God, and which are mere projections of the ego and a constant source of pride. We must not try to penetrate the deep things of God nor seek after esoteric learning through which—save by a miracle—we can scarcely avoid the danger of losing our souls. Nor should we forget the salutary counsel of St. Paul 'not to be more wise than it behoveth to be wise'.[1] Above all we must be on our guard against all exceptional revelations not consistent with the Gospel or with reason, the two rules by which we must always be guided. Even when they appeared to be of divine origin, St. John of the Cross expressed his abhorrence for imaginary visions and 'voices' which afford many souls such satisfaction. For since the coming of Christ, he tells us, all these things are at an end. God no longer reveals Himself directly as He did under the Old Law. But he went still further: he dreaded self-seeking, even in those spiritual states which seem most perfect. And in the Spiritual Canticle he wrote that 'however lofty and sublime may be the communications of the soul with God, and the knowledge of His presence, they are not God in His Essence, nor have they necessarily anything to do with Him. For neither sensible sweetness or divine revelation are clearer testimonies of His presence; nor are dryness or the privation of interior consolation a less clear testimony thereof.' And again: 'It is a clear sign that we love God and are acting for Him when we perform good works equally in times of spiritual aridity or consolation'.

[1] Rom. xii. 3 (Douay).

On the other hand we need not fear that contemplation will lead us into an interior solitude where a sense of self-satisfaction may easily be mistaken for a word spoken to us by God. In *The Ascent of Mount Carmel* we read that 'the characteristic of the truly humble soul is that it dares not treat with God alone'. Contemplation, far from excluding communion with others, calls for it. In Holy Scripture we read: 'Where there are two or three gathered together in my name, there am I in the midst of them'[1]; and in this spirit St. John of the Cross warns us that 'he who follows his own individual line of action will be lukewarm in carrying out even things he has learned from God, until he has first communicated them to his fellow men'. Contemplation only shows its true worth in the action which is its outward evidence, and such action is in turn a means by which it exhorts other souls to share in it.

Here is a maxim which goes beyond both Descartes and Pascal and which, by exalting thought above all created things, obliges it to turn exclusively to God and no longer to creatures. 'The thought of man is worth more than all the world: and therefore God alone is worthy of it.' But the thought of man is only able to turn to God by a movement of love, and the soul lives in the object of its love. The impulse of love thus leads it to share by participation what God possesses by nature. Now God increases His love for the soul in the measure in which the soul increases its love for Him. To do this the soul must be content to accept nothing from creatures and to receive everything from God alone.

The secret of love is that it tends to establish equality between those who love. For one who loves can never be content unless he feels that his love is as great as the love he receives. The effect of love therefore is to transform our will

[1] Matt. xviii. 20 (Douay).

into the very will of God and to teach us instead of remaining
aloof from creatures to rediscover them in God. He has
created all things in an instant and with ease and has left on
each some trace of His existence. He brought all creatures
out of nothingness into being. His bounty enriched them
with all their qualities and all their gifts. Every creature bears
a trace of the footprint of God. The union of our will with
the will of God leads us to look at all created things even
as God looks at them. They are 'the graces of God'. This
attitude of mind should deter us from instituting comparisons
between ourselves and others, or from ever thinking that
others have wronged us and that we are right, or that we
have done more work and are more competent than others.
For there is no poison which brings death so irremediably to
the soul, destroying all the perfection it may previously have
won. We can know that we are making progress only when
we rejoice in the progress of others, choosing rather to be
taught than to teach and content to be shaped and polished
by all.

The soul which has passed through the *Dark Night*, climbed
the slopes of *Mount Carmel*, and is united to God through the
Living Flame of Love, finds rest at last in contemplation, its
purest act. It has reached a state of spiritual peace which is
its highest good, its strength and its light; and, instead of
withdrawing itself from the world, it is able to contemplate
the world in the same light as that in which God regards it;
looking out on it with Him, attentive always to His call to
be with Him in His creative work, and to promote that work.
Not that we can ever be free from anxiety; and no one has
described better than St. John of the Cross the state of the
human soul in which light is in constant struggle with darkness. But if God were to keep the soul always alert and active,
and never ceased to bestow on it new modes of knowledge

and new impulses each more pure and perfect than the last—
the soul would be in the state of glory and no longer in the
state of merit. In this world we have no more than the first
glimpses of that noontide of eternity in which the soul will
give to God all that it receives from Him; while in a mutual
union of will and love all their possessions are now in common. This reciprocal exchange between God and man is
already apparent in the domain of knowledge. St. John of
the Cross adopts the prayer of St. Augustine: 'Let me know
myself, Lord, and I shall know Thee'.[1] And he adds that
according to the teaching of philosophers, one extreme is
clearly known through another. In the spiritual life the soul
lives as though it had gone forth from itself and was raised
above the level of its daily life; yet there is an admirable
coherence between both lives. The soul 'goes about marvel-
ling at the things it sees and hears, which seem to it very
strange and rare, though they are the same which it was
accustomed to experience aforetime'. And in a lovely image
which affords a vivid impression of his profound and lucid
poetry, he compares the soul to a very clear and pure crystal:
'The more degrees of light it receives, the greater concentration of light there is in it and the greater is its enlighten-
ment. And the abundance of light may reach such a point
that it comes to appear to be wholly light and cannot be
distinguished from the light; being enlightened to the greatest
possible extent, it appears to be light itself.' Again he tells us
that God 'is always at the threshold of the soul waiting to
enter even as the rising sun is ready to direct its rays into a
house whose doors are open to receive them'.

It is above all essential for the spiritual man to learn to
keep his soul in peace. Today more than at any other time
men persuade themselves that outward actions alone are of

---

[1] *Noverim me, noverim te, Soliloquies*, II.

real value. Everyone desires to leave his mark upon the world and to measure the strength and quality of his zeal by the outward results he achieves. But we must beware lest we follow the easy way or surrender to vanity: the easy way, because it is always less difficult (whatever people say) to execute a bodily movement than an act of the intelligence (and we are apt to have recourse to the former when we are incapable of the latter); and vanity, because corporal movements are open to all the world; while an act of the intelligence belongs to our secret soul, to our hidden relation with God.

One must be sadly lacking in interior life to confuse peace of soul with idleness. He who possesses this peace of soul must avoid excessive self-reproach, which would deprive him of strength and security. 'He imagines he is doing nothing and wasting his time. But it is no small thing to have suspended activity and desire and the natural operations of his being in order to strip his inward life of all traces of created things and to realize with joy that there is a God who endows his soul with spiritual goods.' The highest state to which it is possible to attain is 'a loving attentiveness to God combined with a great interior peace'.

It would be a serious error to suppose that in the pure love of God the soul experiences nothing more than a movement of sensibility in which it finds rest and satisfaction. True love has its source in the will. In giving preference to movements of sensibility there is always a tendency towards self-seeking against which we must be on our guard. Above all, we must retain control and dominion over our acts so that they may always be accomplished in the light of reason. He who has overcome all the things of this world is said no longer to find joy in their sweetness or sorrow in their bitterness. And by an extraordinary paradox it is also said that the highest state of the soul is that in which it feels neither grief nor emotion;

for the emotion which goes with an act of compassion ceases when the virtue is exercised with a greater degree of perfection. In this state the soul no longer retains the weak element of its virtues: there now remains to it only that which is strong, constant and perfect, as is the case with the angels, who apprehend perfectly things that are grievous without feeling grief, and perform works of mercy and compassion without feeling compassion.

The presence of God is not to be found in those states of disturbance in which the soul experiences a kind of obscure exaltation and imagines that it is transported outside itself; these are the signs of the presence of the body to which we still remain attached with all our strength even when we think we have left it behind. Those who are united to God through a love that is perfect are completely free from such experiences. The presence of God manifests itself in peace of mind and interior joy. The finest passages in St. John of the Cross are those in which he describes the perfect peace of the soul where God abides. 'God', he tells us, 'only bestows His extraordinary graces on souls that are at peace. We must learn to discipline the faculties of the soul and keep them in silence and in stillness so that God may speak.' And again: 'God has only spoken One Word which is His Son and He has spoken It in eternal silence. We must also hearken to His Word in steadfast silence; for God is absolutely hidden in the central point of the soul. The soul must be a walled garden and a sealed-up fountain ready to receive everything from God and nothing from His creatures.' This explains admirably how renunciation of all individual things suffices at one and the same time to purify the soul and to assure the presence of God. 'He that entered in bodily form upon His disciples when the doors were shut will teach us to keep the doors of our faculties—memory, understanding and will—closed against all images of created things.'

6

The essential features of contemplation as they appear in the interior life of St. John of the Cross are the following: If God is always present in the soul (though it is not always in His presence) the first step in the spiritual life must be an effort of purification. This purification rids us of all the preoccupations and particular concepts which form a barrier between God and ourselves, and it throws our souls open to divine illumination and action. Our souls must first be made empty for God to fill them to capacity. But spiritual contemplation is in no way like the contemplation of a material object; for contemplation introduces us to a world without objects, a world of inner activities which it is for us to elicit. The contemplative turns to God by an act which invites the action of God in him. By loving awareness he seeks, not an image of God, but union with Him. And so contemplation is active in essence and constantly elicits fresh acts without any apparent deliberation or choice. In the same way it appears to forsake creatures only to find them again in the will and providence of God.

The spirituality of St. Francis illuminates our daily life by making it translucent, and by showing us in the simplest things and the most insignificant events the marks of God's creative power and the touches of divine grace. St. John of the Cross takes us at once to the apex of the soul—to the ineffable point at which is fulfilled the perfect union of the soul with God, all its old concern for particular things and for other beings which formerly distracted and beguiled it being now discarded and transcended.

St. Francis sees in nature the countenance of God. St. John of the Cross finds it necessary to detach himself from created things in order to rise above them to the invisible and supremely efficacious act of the spirit which gives life and movement to all created things.

It is in the infinite riches of created things that are always in evidence before our eyes, in the endless solicitations that our soul constantly hears and to which it always makes answer, that St. Francis discovers the unity of an abiding Presence. But it is in this same unity stripped of all content and all images that St. John of the Cross seeks at once to fix and establish the life of the spirit.

It is in the totality of the world as it appears before us that St. Francis sees the unity of the Principle which sustains and gives it meaning. It is this unity that St. John of the Cross seeks to attain from the beginning; for it alone will enable us to recapture the totality of things that he fears may distract and enslave us unless, before we turn our attention to created things, we have first established a union of our soul with the Creator, who is above and beyond all the works of creation.

St. John of the Cross always sought to retain this union in purity and perfection. It is on the face of it a high ambition and can only be achieved by profound humility. Such humility does not even dare to ask God to make Himself known. For it is in mystery that He reveals His true presence, and the sense of this presence must never be lost. All our acts must be informed by the consciousness of His presence, and we must not be troubled by our inability ever to do enough of ourselves; for such anxiety often savours of self-love. We must never force our thought, our will or our love; remembering that no particular object must engross our desire if we wish to attain the Good which comprehends and transcends all other goods. Neither must we fear that we are wasting our time so long as we are interiorly united to the Pure Act who is never idle and who is the source of all the acts that can ever take place in time. 'The soul must be convinced of this important truth that, even while it is not aware that it is advancing in the way and by the power of virtue, it is making more progress than if it were consciously in movement under the impulse of its own energy.'

The essential task of the soul is to apprehend the actual presence of God by discarding all images and all individual acts of will directed to particular things. In this way it will find in every existing thing not merely what it is but what God wills it to be. God values the lowest degree of purity of intention above all actions we can do in His service; for of themselves actions do not imply purity of intention; while a pure intention will elicit and outreach our action. To achieve this, we must sever all our attachments, even those whose object is spiritual; for it happens all too often that our desires and the use we make of them find their source and strength in natural appetites. The surest sign that the soul is on a high level of contemplation is that it finds pleasure in being alone with God in simple awareness of Him without any need to exercise the three powers of the soul; for, as we have seen, it suffices if they be directed towards their common principle, detached from particular objects, for them to produce in us acts of faith, hope and charity. In contemplative union all our moral activities find the source of their energy, their unity and their transfiguration.

And if the poetry of St. Francis has taught us through sensible things to attain the spiritual, the poetry of St. John of the Cross has a more secret essence. It is the poetry of a soul which has ceased to take any interest in the things of sense, and which, even in the relation it has with truth, observes a high degree of fastidiousness, as though it were always afraid even at the moment of accepting truth that it might become too attached to it. For all that is necessary is that truth should be alive in us. Yet its action is always obscure; and as Divine Wisdom, in the Canticle of Canticles, says to the soul: 'Turn away thine eyes from me, for they cause me to flee away'.[1]

[1] Canticle of Canticles vi. 4 (Douay).

ST. TERESA: THE UNION OF CONTEMPLATION AND ACTION

THE great saints were types of men and women whom grace transfigured; yet even though they surpass us in the way they responded to grace, they remain none the less within our human compass. They knew our weakness and our affliction; they knew what it was to fail and even to desert the cause, but they never lost faith in the gifts that were given them, and never ceased to believe in the regenerative power of those gifts if better use were made of them. They never gave way to despair. The failings of which they were conscious became the very source of their strength and their humility. The saints are all alike in their total renunciation of self. Through the constant union of their will with the divine will, they were preserved from ever acting entirely of their own motion; and they came to see, even in the most insignificant events, a divine opportunity, a divine call, a design of God's providence, with which they sought to harmonize their actions as closely as possible.

But the saints also differ from one another, as if they were intended, through the infinite varieties of soul and spirit, to show us the infinite variety of the ways that lead to God, in a world where there is no opportunity to start life afresh, though all movements converge towards the one end. And as in our earthly life we choose friends who understand us as we understand them, who reveal us to ourselves, and whose presence never fails to enlighten and enrich us, so there are saints in whom we seem to see ourselves as we would wish to be, who show us the powers and energies of our nature purified and strengthened by spiritual discipline and dedicated to the pursuit of high and holy causes. They show us what God expects of us, the perfection of soul we are always striving to attain, even though we constantly fail and fall again to a lower level.

I

St. Francis of Assisi enables us to understand the miracle of a life in which poverty is transformed into riches and in which nature and grace instead of being in opposition are in harmony, and created things continually show forth the countenance of God. With St. John of the Cross, the poet of contemplation, the spiritual life takes a different form; once more the Nothingness of renunciation gives all things into our possession; but here the vision of the world recedes and fades, leaving only the perfect union of the powers of the soul with God. These powers gradually cease to co-operate with the senses and find in God their purest exercise. Co-operation with the senses keeps us tied to earth; it is a symbol of the powers we exert in the spiritual order and an approach to their exercise. But we cannot fully understand Carmelite spirituality unless we associate St. Teresa of Avila with St. John of the Cross. For in the fulfilment of a destiny at once several and joint, these souls entertained in God the closest and deepest relations; each seemed to become as it were transparent to the other in mutual trust with mutual admiration and a kind of rivalry in holiness.

St. John of the Cross carried meditation on the plane of philosophy to the highest peak where it dissolves in the perfection of mystical union. But St. Teresa had set out to reform her Order; not only, like St. John, did she have to answer for the integrity of her faith to authorities who were uneasy at the very ardour of her spirit; but, also like him, in order to fulfil the vocation which God had given her, she had to face misunderstanding, suspicion, threats and persecution. Her strength, and the indomitable courage with which she used that strength, as well as her utter docility and openheartedness in accepting whatever God asked of her, taught her to endure everything and never to abandon the fight or to acknowledge defeat. Yet she also had to endure the trials inevitably arising within the community for whom she had undertaken to restore the Rule to its original purity. This responsibility weighed on her, soul and body, and constantly gave rise to fresh preoccupations in the material and the spiritual order. She was continually harassed by petty and ever-recurring cares which overwhelmed and exhausted her. But the interior light of the divine presence which never left her—even when it gave no outward sign—sustained her in all, even the least of her activities.

Yet she did not escape the anguish which always accompanies the influence we exert on others who, even when they have accepted a rule of religious life, excite our apprehension lest either through lack or excess of zeal, they may not live up to their rule, or come to follow it in the letter rather than the spirit. We fear lest they may fail to discover within themselves the interior impulse, at once personal and spiritual, which gives meaning and fruitfulness to a religious rule of life; or that they may be too ready to yield submission to it on the very occasions when we would wish it to be a principle of liberation. And what are we to say of all those movements of self-love which in the relation between one soul and another, or between the soul and God, so often insinuate themselves into the movements of charity and faith so that it is often difficult to identify them, and to realize the menace they always are to our spiritual integrity?

No one knew better than St. Teresa all the petty and tiresome obstacles that hinder our efforts to transform the visible world—all the opposition that arises from habit, opinion and vanity, whenever we try to restore to its first principle any movement of the spiritual life which, from contact with the world, finds its original purity gradually deteriorating. She knew also all the contradictions which have to be mastered when we seek to harmonize the aspirations of our deepest personal life with the claims of life in community; or when we seek to reconcile our urgent call to a life devoted to God with those indispensable material conditions that are always apt to check and hinder it. St. Teresa had to confront all these difficulties at the same time; but far from looking on them as obstacles interrupting her activity and distracting her from the high plane of contemplation where her spirit habitually dwelt, they became for her an experience and proof of contemplation, and a testimony to its efficacy and worth—perhaps even the only way in which she was permitted to put contemplation into practice.

The lesson that St. Teresa teaches us is that contemplation and action are indissolubly united. No one mounted to greater heights on the ladder of contemplation than she; yet at the same time no one condescended more closely to all the immediate and concrete obligations that life imposes. Perhaps we ought to say that in her case the two movements were really one. Otherwise contemplation would be in danger of becoming academic and barren, while action would be material and blind. At the point where they converge, Martha and Mary become identified.

But the example of St. Teresa does more than teach us to reflect on the union of contemplation and action; it also invites us, as we study the life of this remarkable woman, to consider the essential part that women have been called upon to play in the shaping of the spiritual life. It is in men that we best observe the divorce between contemplation and action, as though the activity of man tended always to specialization, and the division of labour was a law of man's nature. But women even in our own day follow a routine of work which is nearer to the sources of life, and calls for a greater and deeper energy of love to sustain its spontaneous dedication to the humble and familiar tasks of daily life. Martha and Mary are both of them women; but we are surprised that they should not be identical, that they should have divided between them tasks which cannot really be separated, and which it is the vocation of women to combine. Mary has the better part, for Martha cannot live by bread alone; but Mary is not obliged in all circumstances to reject the complaint that Martha makes.

The example of St. Teresa invites us to reflect on the part that women play in the Christian community. St. Jane Frances de Chantal tells us that 'women need little learning but great humility, simplicity and love'. St. Teresa shows us the rôle that must be played by gentleness, tenderness and enthusiasm in the spiritual life. The virtues of Mary the Mother of God are a model for all. An English writer who was struck by the part played by women in the Gospel makes this comment on certain texts of St. Luke: 'When the Saviour was born women rejoiced in Him before either men or angels'; and he adds that he never read of a man who had given as much as two pennies to Our Lord, whereas women followed Him and helped Him with their substance. 'It was a woman who bathed His feet with tears, and a woman who anointed His body for burial; women wept for Him as He made His way to Calvary; women followed Him after He was taken down from the Cross, and sat by the sepulchre where He was buried. . . . Women were with Him on the morning of His resurrection, and first brought to His disciples the news that He had risen from the dead.'

II

St. Teresa was born in 1515 of a noble family at Avila in Castile, the country of Don Quixote. Her brothers went to America with the Conquistadors and two met their death fighting with them in Peru. To her origin perhaps was due the exceptional ardour of her nature, the courage and indomitable strength with which she faced every obstacle and the devotion to the Absolute which stamped all her enterprises with serene assurance and unyielding resolution. But the hero of Cervantes showed a courage entirely of the human order; the real continually eluded him, because his generous soul enveloped everything in the mists of his imagination and he failed to make any distinction between the things he saw and the things he fancied. To distinguish with certitude what men have done from what they ought to have done, we must be able to rise to the Supreme Principle on whom all created things depend. It does not therefore surprise us to find in St. Teresa a powerful realism which enabled her to perceive the wretchedness of our human condition in such a direct, startling and sometimes ruthless way. Her remarkable idealism on the other hand (one may almost call it a realism of the spiritual order the object of which was infinitely high) inspired her belief that nothing was impossible if one had perfect faith and entire confidence in the will of God and in the gifts He bestows on us; for such gifts are always in proportion to what He asks of us.

In her youth St. Teresa read many romances which were calculated to be a source of early satisfaction to a spirit destined soon to turn in quite a different direction. She was full of simplicity and gaiety, spontaneous and independent, with a quick wit and ready repartee. To Fray Juan de la Miseria who had just painted her portrait she said: 'God forgive me, Brother John, but you have made me look ugly and blear-eyed'. Although she appeared to be strong, she suffered almost continually from ill-health; but she soon learnt to make the best of things, and of her health she said: 'Although it is always bad, I am much better since I have ceased to take so much care of it'. She neglected none of the duties proper to her sex, and was an excellent needlewoman. But she was continually overburdened with business matters and could devote but little time to other pursuits.

At the age of twenty she entered the Carmelite Convent of the Incarnation at Avila, and there for about twenty-seven years she lived in the observance of the Mitigated Rule. The rigour of the Rule had been tempered because it was thought to be too hard to keep, but in mitigating it a measure of laxity had crept in. St. Teresa was to show that rules and prescriptions, which seem harsh and oppressive when faith is weak, become tolerable and even necessary when faith is ardent, and instead of oppressing us they then become a source of strength and support. There is no doubt that the task of St. Teresa, who acted in obedience to a divine inspiration which she found irresistible, was to revive faith which had grown listless. The sole object of all the foundations she instituted was to provide the material means for reviving faith by restoring the necessary instruments which had gradually become worn and slack. All the burdens she bore, all the censures she incurred, all the risks she ran were measured and accepted in advance. She knew that there is a danger of the spiritual life remaining no more than a dream or aspiration of the individual soul unless it can find, in an organization which gives it substance and direction, a means of proving and expressing itself in real life; of attaining, in a life lived in community, something more than the form of self-seeking we are apt to mistake for the search for God. St. Teresa undertook the reform of her Order at the age of forty-seven when our powers are at their height, when our experience is mature and when we set forth on the road that still lies before us, and are conscious that our destiny is now being decided. The reform of her Order was to be the cause of all her agony of mind. On our part, we are apt to cling to old habits because of the peace they bring. We reject the

demands that great souls make upon us to examine our whole
life, as firmly as if they called on us to rise from the dead.
Such great souls always begin to make us uneasy. And we are
often at a loss to distinguish between a revolution which
obliges us to build, and one whose only purpose is to destroy.
It is therefore not surprising to find St. Teresa's first Superiors
treating her as a 'restless gadabout'. She spent her whole life
defending herself against accusations. She was continually
under suspicion; she was thrown into prison. But persecution, far from discouraging her, served only to strengthen
her fortitude and gave her a more vivid and lively sense of
the presence of God; it united her more closely with Christ
in His Passion and continued to bring her fresh grace. It made
the reform of her Order—to which she had consecrated and
sacrificed her whole self in advance—appear to be more than
ever necessary.

The example of St. Teresa admirably illustrates how often
the greatest things that are accomplished in the world have
the humblest beginnings; it is God who brings them to
maturity and makes them bear fruit. In whatever state we
have been placed by God the important thing is to respond
faithfully to His call, never to bargain with Him, and always
be ready to give ourselves entirely to Him without reservation. And this simple nun from Avila, by the sole ardour of
her spirit, radiated in her convent the spiritual flame that
burned within her—a flame she was destined at the price of
much labour and mortification gradually to spread throughout Spain, and from which all Christian souls would receive
an increase of light and love.

St. Teresa found to hand a mighty source of strength
in certain souls she met upon her way. Their vocation
differed from hers, but like her they knew the perfection
of a constant union of the soul with God. There was
first St. John of the Cross whom she met when he was

only twenty-five and she was fifty-two. She used to call him her Seneca, small in stature but great in the eyes of God. He raised the science of mystical contemplation to a higher point than any other saint. But St. Teresa did not hesitate, with a kind of rough but tender familiarity, to bring him back to the things of earth, as if it were there that contemplation must justify its claims. 'May the Lord deliver me', she said, 'from people who are so spiritual that they wish to turn everything to perfect contemplation, come what may.' Then there was St. Peter of Alcantara, one of the most rigorous of all ascetics, who found that the hardest penance of all was to resist sleep; and who only allowed himself one-and-a-half hours' sleep, while sitting up. This was certainly not an example to be proposed for imitation by anyone; but in the infinite variety of spiritual vocations it serves to remind us to our shame of all the comforts with which we too often surround our bodies and, on the other hand, of all the resources at the disposal of our will, which enable us to resist and to reject such habits of ease. But St. Teresa did not frame rules on such a model either for herself or for those in her charge. We are moved with admiration for the broadmindedness she displayed both in her judgement and her conduct; for though all her actions were governed by reason, wisdom and a sense of proportion, she never ceased to derive strength and ardour from those extreme types of the spiritual life from whom we learn that there is nothing in our human state which cannot be transcended and supernaturalized, and that all our enterprises have their source and end in the Absolute.

The last part of St. Teresa's life is full of instruction for us, for it shows in an astonishing way what was certainly the deep significance and even the essence of her destiny on earth—that is, the most close and perfect union of contemplation and action that has ever been achieved. It is as though she were sent to show us that it is equally wrong to regard these two aspects of life as mutually incompatible, either by exalting the contemplative life as self-sufficient, or by turning to the active life, for fear that in contemplation there may lurk a cult of self, leading to spiritual inactivity and impotence. Towards the end of her life St. Teresa seems to have experienced a profound, constant and celestial peace. Yet her life was more prolific than ever in business affairs, journeys, labour and suffering. It was as if the two sides of our nature had found in her their proper exercise; as if our temporal existence received all its power and all its light from our spiritual being, at the price of discharging a painful and wearisome task, so that the spirit might find peace, security and joy. The life of St. Teresa admirably illustrates the union between these two sides of our nature, one of which must be ready to accept and endure fresh trials, in order that the other may transmute them into new sources of peace and love. This idea finds expression in the charming story of the almond-tree which is said to have flowered in October at the time of her death. We are also told that whenever her tomb was opened her body was found to be supple and fragrant.

III

The writings of St. Teresa cannot be separated from her life. Her most important work, her *Life* (*Vida*), is at the same time part of her *Acta*. Unlike most professional writers, she wrote her book under obedience; and to us it is all the more moving since she was ordered to write it not so much for the edification of others as to justify herself: by this book in fact she was to be judged and perhaps condemned. We can readily understand with what anxiety she composed it. But it has no trace of calculation or of fear; it is marked by such firmness and assurance, such confidence in her own good cause and in the mission she had been given, such straightforwardness and simplicity, such faith and enthusiasm, that it seems to have been written not so much to exonerate her as to stir and convert us. The admiration that Fr. Diego de Yanguas had for it led him to say—in the imaginative and homely language so common among Spaniards—that 'when he was about to celebrate the Holy Sacrifice he first warmed himself at this brazier'. St. Teresa calls this *Life* her great book. For twelve years it remained in the hands of the Inquisition, and for this reason she was led to write *The Interior Castle*, where she describes the outer court and mansions which reflect the different levels of consciousness, or the different stages of the soul's ascent to God. The book is in fact the record of her whole life. She wrote it in three months at the age of sixty-two at the bidding of her confessor. And what a model it is for those who write only from self-love, or to paint a flattering portrait of themselves or to acquire a reputation which will add to their importance. To write under obedience is to write only because the occasion demands it, in response to an interior urge which is irresistible. But observe with what unconcern and apparent lack of care she sets about her task, as though it were distracting her from her rightful occupations. She tells us that she wrote by stealth and under difficulties, and never had time to revise what she had written. She lent an attentive ear to the interior voices of her own sincerity and of divine inspiration, without making any distinction between them, so steadfastly was her gaze directed towards God in peaceful and quiet confidence. Before starting to write she neither knew what she was going to say nor how she would say it. Yet how much better she writes than others who are so concerned about saying the right thing. It is just the absence of preparation in her writing that brings her so vividly before us and shows forth to all the world the faith which shines in her and the love which ravishes her soul.

We must not forget, however, that St. Teresa was a woman who passed her life among women; and she was always haunted by the problem: by what double discipline, exterior and interior, was it possible to promote the highest spiritual development in women living in a community? She knew that men excelled in knowledge, and women excelled in love. But she also knew how difficult it is to get to know women—much more so than their confessors imagine. Mark this text in which she takes these confessors to task in the light of her experience, with robust good sense and humour: 'You surprise me by saying that you have only to see this young woman to know what she is like. Women-folk are not so easy to get to know. Even when you have heard their confessions for several years, you will be surprised to find how little you have understood them; for they do not understand themselves well enough to declare their faults, and yet you judge them just by what they say.' Listen to her as she draws up the rules for entry into the community: 'Do not think that enthusiasm or external signs are enough, or the unshakable belief that each postulant has in the reality of her vocation. The qualities that are needed are more ordinary but more solid.' 'Our Constitution', she says, 'forbids us to receive young women who lack judgement.' There is a warning too, as one might expect, not to trust solemn, austere or melancholy airs which are often mistaken for marks of genuine piety. She prefers girls with gaiety and spirit, and observes wittily: 'In our Rule we have no use for austere people: the Rule itself is quite austere enough'.

One would expect her to give priority to those exceptional states of which she herself had so direct and vivid an experience, when the whole capacity of our soul is filled (as it seems) no longer by us, but by God. She gives an admirable description of visions and of 'ecstasies to which I am sure that I contribute about as much as if I were the stump of a tree. . . . I seem to see nothing, to say nothing, to have no power of willing; but within me is a spirit which animates, guides and sustains me. . . . One sees nothing either inwardly or outwardly, since the soul does not dwell in the imagination. But though it sees nothing, and though no particular thing is present to the senses, the soul is conscious of its object and its whereabouts more clearly than if it saw. Without the aid of any interior or any exterior word one is conscious of a Presence nearby.' Though the operation of the senses is suspended, St. Teresa recognizes the working of a secret grace which is outside the comprehension of ordinary folk. And she invokes the saying of St. Paul: 'The sensual man perceiveth not these things that are of the Spirit of God'.[1] But far from encouraging the pursuit of sensible favours and extraordinary ways, she was always on her guard against them, treating them rather as signs of weakness common among women, for which a remedy has to be found. 'Women are weak', she says, 'and always liable to mistake the figments of their imagination for true visions.' And she adds with a robustness of thought that seems singularly bold: 'Visions of themselves are neither good nor evil: their good or evil depends on the use we make of them. Even if they are from God they can still be evil if we let them minister to our vanity or persuade us that we are holy. When they are from the devil they can still be good if they humble us with the thought that they are from God and that we are unworthy of them.' We can judge by the clearness and certitude of such teaching how strongly she reacted against all forms of illuminism at a time when, even more than today, subjective exaltation so often appeared in the guise of mysticism. Although St. Teresa was so ardent and had risen to such heights of contemplation and had received such rare graces, she judged these things by a purely Cartesian mode of reasoning. But she knew

---

[1] 1 Cor. ii. 14 (Douay).

that divine gifts and graces always presuppose, and never do more than transform, our natural faculties.

On the other hand, woman though she was, and although she recognized that women excel in intuition and in love, she declined to claim any advantage from this. She had no desire that they should invoke the weakness of their sensitive nature as a sign of their spiritual perfection. She always reacted with a fine scorn against a temptation of this kind: 'I never remember having wept even in my greatest afflictions, for God gave me a strength of soul which is rare in women.' And Fr. Salinas said of her: 'She is a man of the bearded sort'. No one ever heard her utter a word of complaint. 'I am not a woman of that sort: I have a stout heart.' She admits that the thought of being a woman took all the heart out of her. Again she is a true woman in knowing that she is a woman without wishing to be one. She desired all her daughters to love a valiant spirit as she did. And she said to them: 'I do not want you to trade on your womanhood. You must be as strong as the strongest of men: and if you do what lies in you to do, I promise you that Our Lord will give you such strength that men will marvel at you.' Words of such incomparable spirit show us that at the highest point of the soul and in face of the loftiest demands of the spiritual life the differences that count are not those that spring from nature but those only which spring from inner resolve and a passion for the Absolute. The Saint's words anticipate those spoken by the indomitable Jacqueline Pascal in circumstances of much peril: 'There may be occasions when, if bishops show no more courage than young girls, it is the duty of young girls to show the courage of bishops'.

IV

If we seek to identify the essential features which distinguished this great saint, we shall find that she excelled in resolution and daring; she derived all her strength, confidence and zest, all her inflexible resolution in time of trial and danger, from her constant sense of the presence of God. No one knew better than she how to combine boldness in idea, hazard in enterprise, prudence and patience in execution. Listen to her cry: 'One may die, to be sure, but be defeated—never'. She was prepared to meet every challenge. 'I think I should be ready to take on the whole host of Lutherans single-handed. For we can do all in Christ.' She was never disturbed by fear, for God was always by her side, bearing her up. He would say to her: 'Fear not, it is I'. 'It seems to me', she declared, 'that it is no longer I who am living, speaking, willing; but within me there is One who guides and strengthens me.' She never refused any task on the ground of her own weakness, for if God required her to do it, she knew He would give her the strength to carry it through. 'O Lord, my God, how clear it is that you are all-powerful! We must not hesitate to do the things you ask for—however impossible they seem, if we judge them according to nature—because you make it possible to do them. All that is necessary is to love you with our whole heart and to renounce all else for your love.' It is not surprising to hear her quoting with admiration the words of St. Augustine: 'Give me, O Lord, the strength to do what you command, and then command me to do what you will'.

From whatever angle we study the life of St. Teresa we shall find that the root and principle of all her actions was an intense and constant awareness of the presence of God. This awareness made her say she had no fear that the devil would deceive her or that anyone in the world would undeceive her. It also explains why her vigorous personality always adopted an attitude of detachment in affirming her point of view. She insists that humility must always come first, for the strength we need can never come through our own resources. But she had no use for the false humility that makes us hide our gifts and by so doing slight the Giver of all good things. We must learn to recognize all the graces God has given us, and acknowledge that we in no way deserve them. We must do more, and transform the self-love which binds us to ourselves into a feeling of gratitude towards God who has created us. What can be more simple, more artless and more touching than her prayer: 'However useless I may be and however unprofitable to others, I will never cease to praise you, O my God, for having made me just as I am'. In this way our very weakness becomes a means of leading us back to God, and of finding even in our littleness the sign of His power and His love.

The experience St. Teresa had of God put her above and beyond philosophers and theologians. 'If God Himself had not been my teacher', she said, 'all my reading would have brought me little knowledge.' Reading was actually a difficulty for her, for, whenever she tried to read, her reading at once gave way to prayer. Her knowledge was of divine origin, an experimental knowledge which is of no worth unless it becomes a rule of life and action. And so we can understand why even her directors put themselves under her direction. She showed how contemplation could pass into action, infusing into it force and light, so that it became an example of spiritual activity, inviting wonder and imitation on all sides. But St. Teresa never overlooked the rule of prudence which, in community life, obliges us to take into consideration even the humblest vocations, and which protects simple souls from being discouraged by outstanding examples of spiritual perfection on a level they are never likely to approach. St. Teresa applied to herself the rule—so well suited to her daughters in their relations with her—that we must always make a clear distinction between what we can imitate, and what we can only admire. But if there is one kind of imitation which will deflect us from what we are required to do and from the duties we have to perform, there is another kind, having its source in admiration, which enables us in our proper sphere and with our own particular gifts, to achieve the same victory over ourselves and the same degree of spiritualization of all our powers as the greatest souls attain on a plane above our own.

St. Teresa invites us also to reflect upon the principles of religious life which enable us, in a more perfect manner, and in conditions of particular privilege, to accomplish the task common to all in the wider setting of social life, which is to become mediators one for another. As there are societies for the pursuit of pleasure, so there are societies for the pursuit of holiness. In these, St. Teresa tells us, friendships must be knit between persons of established virtue. She is fully aware that increase of charity springs from communion with others. She loved her Order with a true passion, and she specially loved the individual life spent face to face with God, and the common quest for Him in community which are the very essence of the religious life. Like St. Clare, she taught that poverty and humility are like a high wall which shuts us away from the world and encloses us within ourselves. And lest the diversity in the forms of religious life should elude us, we must not forget that St. Teresa did not wish her nuns to beg. 'It is a rule of our Constitution never to beg, save in great necessity.' She says that if through overanxiety alms were accepted on one or two occasions, it might soon become a habit. 'And we might then beg for something not strictly necessary from people who need it more than we do.' She wished her nuns to preserve the spirit of poverty while avoiding the peril of seeking alms. And yet, like the disciples of St. Francis, she held that poverty contains within itself all the good things of this world, and that to despise the world is to be master of it. This mastery, she thought, could best be achieved by withdrawal from the world, for such withdrawal would break down all the barriers between the soul and God. She treasured the cloistered life above all things. 'One must have experienced it', she tells us, 'to understand what joy our foundations gave us especially when we were in an enclosure which denied access to lay persons; for, though we loved them dearly, no consolation equalled that of being in community alone.' Even Leibniz admired the inner state of soul which disposed St. Teresa to look at things as though God and she were alone in the world. What happiness such a separation brings; for, instead of fixing us in isolation from our fellow-creatures, it is a unique means of bringing their presence near to us, and overcoming our separation by enabling us to attain the Supreme Principle in whom they enjoy communion among themselves and with us.

It was because her gaze was always directed towards God that St. Teresa was delivered from all the false scruples which cause the ego to concentrate on itself and brood continually on its own imperfections. 'Do not imagine', she warns us, 'that a mere thought is sinful, however evil it may be.' A thought becomes sinful only when we begin to entertain it and give way to it. It was the vision of God which made her indifferent to the opinions of others. We must not care whether people speak well or ill of us and must take no more notice of criticism levelled at us than if it were aimed at someone else. Let others defend us: this is not our concern. It was her vision of God again which, instead of detaching her from nature, helped her to find the Creator in His creation— to admire the beauty in meadow and stream, in the simplicity of a child and even in the humblest gifts bestowed on her.

v

There was in the life of St. Teresa an unparalleled vigour, keenness and actuality because for her, life had meaning only in its relation to eternity. For it is eternity which fills our years, making our life a period of expectation, and thus giving light and significance to each of the events that make up our history. The sense of eternity was of long standing with St. Teresa. She recalls the emotion she felt, when, as children, she and her brother used to think about everlasting reward and punishment: they used to repeat the words 'for ever . . . for ever'. Most of us think of time with unutterable anguish: for its flight is something we cannot arrest, something in which our life seems to vanish away while there is nothing we can do to hold it back. The shortness of our span of life, the certainty that it will end one day, the fear that we may have failed to make good use of it, the sense that we are leaving behind us nothing but emptiness and waste of days, all this causes us grief and affliction. How different is the outlook of St. Teresa. Eternity, not time, is the object of her thought, affection and desire. She is unlike those who live only for the passing hour, who see in each event nothing beyond the actual moment in which it happens, for whom the past is always the object of remembrance and regret, who always run to meet the coming hour and count the slow-paced minutes as they pass. For St. Teresa there was a kind of equality between the successive moments of time. Each of these makes its own demand on us, to which we can respond only if we are able to raise ourselves to the Eternal Presence. For this reason she attached little importance to dates and the computation of time. She was not interested in the relation between days and months and years. All her attention was focused on the relation of each phase of time with eternity. But when she did stop to consider the actual passage of time, she did not find eternity in it here and now, but saw time rather as a barrier separating her from eternity, an obstacle which obliged her to wait. Hence the consoling reflection which moved her to say: 'What comes to an end is always brief'. Hence too her frequent sense of time passing away so quickly that there was no time to do anything. But, when she thinks of death as the gateway to eternity, she laments for the opposite reason: 'How slow this life is, and how painful our exile'. Hence the sublime strength which drives her to link death with life, making life itself a kind of death; for life keeps death at bay—the death that will bring her eternal life. Finally there are her famous and lovely words: 'Waiting crucifies me and makes me suffer so greatly that I die because I do not die'. These words throw into sharp relief the tragic oscillation in our own souls between being and not-being, our sensitive soul being obliged to deny itself so that through its death our spiritual being may come to life.

The example of St. Teresa is of inestimable value in teaching us how contemplation and action are really indistinguishable. To us they seem to be separate and mutually contradictory, and we wonder how they can possibly be reconciled. Contemplation is truly action at the high point of the soul where it takes place and towards which it urges us always to ascend. For St. Teresa there is no alternating elevation and descent of the soul from the humblest tasks in the material order to the most sublime graces of prayer. In contemplation the humble and the sublime are one. He who has risen to the greatest heights in the spiritual life performs the most commonplace actions with the greatest perfection. Always to keep our thoughts on a high level, she says, is a great encouragement in bringing our actions to the same level. 'God alone suffices'; because it is He who gives unity to our life. His will is that the life of mysticism and the life of action should each nourish the other; that solitude should help us to communicate with all creatures and that, even in the extremity of suffering, we should be able to experience the fullness of joy.

But God never allows us to despise the human means He has placed in our hands and which He wishes us to use. All our actions—though these depend for their success on God alone—must be performed in accordance with the laws of our reason. The best biographer of St. Teresa expresses admiration for her wisdom, her ripe and balanced judgement, her habit of considering carefully whatever she had to do; of weighing with careful deliberation all the pros and cons of the matter in hand. Once she had taken a decision, she pursued her course of action with the utmost fidelity. In her prayers she had recourse to God as the source of all prudence: 'Grant that I may know how to use my reason to judge and weigh everything in a true balance, so as to render to each one what is his due. And may I ever be on my guard in distinguishing the better from the worse and make the right choice with true purity of intention.'

Union with God always starts with a state of simple re-collection; but it will transform all the powers of our soul by laying bare their spiritual operation, and at the same time induce a state of perfect tranquillity into which those same powers enter and find repose. Union with God provides unending consolation, for it makes us realize that nothing can happen apart from the will of God, and that no one is tempted beyond what he can bear. This gives the soul a sense of confidence and security, and raises it far above the strife between love of self and the love of God which showed it had so far failed to find Him. Mark the quiet courage with which St. Teresa speaks of the path that leads to Him. 'I do not know, Lord, how the road that leads to You can be called narrow. To me it seems not a path, but a King's high-way; and the greater our courage in setting out upon our journey, the more confidently we shall travel the road. You are always there to raise up those who stumble; and not one fall, nor even many falls, will make us lose our soul, so long as we are free from worldly desires and have given You our hearts and follow You in the way of humility.' God, she reminds us, often allows us to fall in order to teach us humility, and when we pick ourselves up with a right intention, realizing our own weakness, we can derive from that same fall new strength to advance in the way of the Lord.

We must not suppose that for St. Teresa contemplation was necessary for salvation. To many pure souls with no experience of contemplation, such a belief might cause despair. Contemplation is a gift of God but something He does not require of all of us. It is even possible that in a fruitless attempt to attain it, we may wander from our true path. We must not forget that he who thinks he is only on the lowest rung of the ladder may in the sight of God have reached the top. The union required of us by God is not the union of contemplation, but the union of our will; that is to say, a state in which the soul is detached from all worldly things and wishes for nothing that is out of harmony with the will of God; in which our will, being entirely conformed to His will, and wholly absorbed in Him, no longer retains any trace of self-love or love of any created thing. The soul is now so completely oblivious of all self-interest that it seems no longer to have any existence of its own, for it has become one with God. It now enjoys ineffable peace and has no need to reflect in order to apprehend the presence of God. It desires neither death nor life. And so love, by liberating us from the things of earth and by allowing us to soar above them, makes us masters of all the elements and of the world itself; and it is humility which restores the true relation between our nothingness and the Perfect Being of God.

V

ST. FRANCIS DE SALES: THE UNITY OF WILL AND LOVE

I

OF all the saints none seems closer to the world and therefore nearer to us than St. Francis de Sales. Yet no saint penetrates more deeply into the secret places of our hearts. By seeking out what we desire as distinct from what we appear to desire, he reveals to us what we really are. He reconciles us to ourselves through the continuity there is between the state of our soul and the end it seeks to attain. Far from setting up an intolerable separation between that which is within us and the object to which we aspire, he shows us that this object is already present within us, and that what we have to do is to lay hold of it. He teaches us to bear with our individual nature instead of disowning it; to find in it not an obstacle to be overcome, and a source of discouragement, but a power we must make respond to a spiritual inspiration of which it bears the sign and feels the attraction. While others direct our attention merely to our own impotence, St. Francis de Sales urges us to discover within ourselves a source of infinite power; so that our will, by a simple act of interior assent, is able to open a way for its exercise instead of impeding its activity or paralysing its effect. He is the very model of the spiritual director whom we seek or would wish to be in our own regard. At no time does he impose any constraint that appears to come from outside: all he asks is that we should enter more deeply into our secret selves. No one has ever analysed more fully the movements of desire; he never seems to oppose these movements; he appears on the contrary to accept and enter into them. But he gets down to their very source which we often fail to perceive: and seeks to guide them to their proper end, which we constantly tend to forget because we allow our desires to rest on particular objects none of which is able to satisfy us. His remarkable achievement in describing the working of our conscience is twofold: he makes this tend wholly in the direction of our desires and brings us at the same time into the closest contact with our counsellor, till it is impossible to tell which of us it is that is involved, since each makes the other what he is by the same act, the act which distinguishes us yet makes us one. And we are all so bound up together that none of us is free from responsibility for other souls as well as for his own. How indeed can we distinguish the responsibility we assume in our own regard from the responsibility we assume in regard to others? Whenever two souls meet we must recognize, as this great saint did, that to teach and to learn is for each of them one single experience.

Now whether we consider the *Introduction to the Devout Life* or the *Treatise on the Love of God*, whether St. Francis is addressing Philothea or Theotimus, it is clear that the composition of a purely theoretical work was beyond him. He needed the stimulus of another soul to whom he might communicate the fruit of his experience. It is as if he required an imaginary presence (always perhaps concealing a real personality) to bring to life within him the spring of love which comes from God and returns to Him, but only after having flowed between creatures. There is in St. Francis a feminine tenderness which has often been noted and which is shown in his choice of words and in his use of such images as those taken from flowers or honey. This tenderness may have found its expression also in the close ties which united him to St. Jane de Chantal and in his constant preoccupation with the spiritual affairs of the Visitation nuns. It would seem that in all the forms of love there is a threefold character of gentleness, ardour and surrender, of which women are the vehicle and the model. Mary the Mother of God is inseparable from the idea of Christian love; while the individual soul in its relation to God, loves and is loved, even as Mary loved and was loved by her Son.

But it would be a great mistake to think that love, according to St. Francis, amounts to nothing more than a movement of the sensitive nature to which all our interior powers need only surrender in silence. No one perhaps ever combined firmness and gentleness as he did. Indeed it is hard to imagine a more lucid and vigorous mind, or one who had such confidence in the will, or so steady a resolve to dominate and direct all the spontaneous movements of nature instead of allowing them to dominate him. No one ever had a more virile conscience; it was thoroughly able to rule itself and steadfastly refused to yield to the play of emotion or the uncertainties of chance. Yet for all his constant preoccupations with the actual relations between individual souls, and the circumstances, capacity and vocation of each, he was concerned, among all the forms of love, with one alone, namely, the love which leads us to God. All human love seemed valueless and devoid of meaning for him save in so far as it was at once a symbol and an expression of the love God has for His creatures; for creation itself is nothing more than an act of love, and the love that creatures have for God is only a reflection of the love that God has for them.

Nothing can give us greater strength and consolation especially at the present day than the works of St. Francis de Sales. For his teaching is completely opposed to those doctrines of contemporary thought which only stress the unhappiness of mankind in face of all its continual misfortunes. In fact all these doctrines involve a dualism, and even an inescapable contradiction between existence as we know it, and the spiritual aspirations within us which our actual existence constantly belies. These modern thinkers would have us believe that this existence, with its limitations, its sufferings and its attendant misery is the only reality; and that the spirit is nothing but an ineffectual and illusory activity which never becomes incarnate, that is, never comes to life; it can never transform existence: it can only degrade it. St. Francis sees things quite differently; for him it is in the life of the spirit alone that each of us achieves the self-awareness which is our authentic mode of existence. The soul must therefore be taught not to mistrust itself, and by means of an inward act, all too often omitted, it must maintain its interior purity which is always in peril. It must not allow itself to be deterred or discouraged by the external obstacles by which it is confronted; it must learn to find in nature not only a source of inexhaustible beauty but also an instrument and guide for its own operation. It must learn to see in the limitations that are imposed on it the conditions of its progress, and to interpret the sufferings it has to endure as so many trials which lead to a deeper understanding of events and distil for us their spiritual meaning. Must we say that such an undertaking is foredoomed to failure? That might be so if the spirit abandoned the struggle in advance; if it acknowledged the world to be too strong; if it were resigned to be but a pale reflection of that world; and finally if it were false to its deepest essence, which resides not in knowledge but in love; and if it failed to see that all its powers are measured by its power to love; for in the measure in which love is exercised, it justifies the world, and in the measure in which it is withdrawn, the world is lost.

II

The theory of love is at the heart of all the teaching of St. Francis de Sales. The *Treatise on the Love of God* is a kind of testament of love. We may find it long-winded and repetitive, but this is true of life itself, which is nothing more than love in action. In this book St. Francis studies all the aspects of our individual life, all the situations in which we find ourselves, all our relations with our fellow-men, all our sorrows, all our joys. These he scrutinizes in the pure light of love, according as love shines through or is obscured in each, making its sheer presence the single standard of judgement. But what exactly do we mean by love? It is our very being, inasmuch as our being resides in an interior movement inclining it towards the Good, a good which we make our own good. No one can deny that love is the core of our being, and that happiness or unhappiness depends on whether this love is frustrated or fulfilled.

But is not love at the same time a gift that has been bestowed on us? This is perhaps the token of its transcendence, in origin and end. It seems that love does not depend on us, either in its birth or its fulfilment; and that it breaks down all the barriers that might have seemed to limit our action. So long as we are lacking in love we are immured within the solitude of individual existence, and love alone can set us free. Love plunges us into a world without limits where we are at the same time within and yet outside ourselves. And by a strange paradox we only seem to reach the heart of our being through a movement which takes us beyond ourselves. In other words all love comes from God and returns to Him. There is indeed no love but the love of God: that is the indissoluble union of His unfailing love for us, and the love we have for Him in which we almost always fall short. Such love alone is able to justify our existence and the entire work of creation, and for one who has experience of it problems cease to exist. But no one experiences it at all times, or with equal ardour. It is inevitable that the self should fail sometimes; and there is nothing that may not become an object of scandal, even the whole universe, if we fail to look on it with love. The mystery of love is that it changes nothing in the world, which continues to exhibit the same abominations and sufferings; yet it has the power to suffuse these things with an invisible and supernatural light. When love reigns, suffering is invested with new meaning, and is relieved and slowly transformed into a joy of another order.

The core of the whole doctrine of love, and perhaps the deepest secret of our souls, lies in the relation that is established between will and love. It would seem at first that these two faculties are mutually opposed and even contradict one another. For will depends upon ourselves; it resides in an initiative within our control, and in a sense it isolates us both from nature and from God, leaving our destiny in our own hands. Love, on the other hand, surges up within us in spite of ourselves; without waiting for our consent it takes possession of us and subdues us to its service. And this happens not only in human love which is ruled by our instinct and the law of our members, but also in divine love, where grace seems to take and carry us away, leaving us no option but to follow. In each case the will must remain mute. For as soon as it becomes active, the ego asserts itself and offers resistance to love. Love comes to us from outside; it has no need of the will, and indeed renders it impotent and useless. And so in human love, the will always puts up a struggle and is often defeated; or, if it succeeds in holding its own, it is because it rises to the level of true heroism. In divine love it resists the impulsion of grace, and often successfully, as though grace itself depended for its efficacy on the interior consent which the will in such cases refuses to give. These two opposite effects of the will seem to demonstrate its independence in regard to love. When it strives against instinct and against grace, the will is exerting its independent power; for in the one case it declines to accept anything from nature, while in the other it refuses the help that is offered from on high.

These are precisely the antimonies that St. Francis de Sales seeks to overcome. He teaches us not to look upon nature and grace as contraries. For like St. Francis of Assisi he held that nature comes from God. We can do nothing without nature; and its dynamism is a power given to us that we may make good use of it. But we misuse our nature whenever we treat it as self-sufficient and as an end fulfilling itself in the satisfaction of selfish impulses which have meaning only if they are sublimated and spiritualized. Egoist impulses become obstacles in our way when they seek wholly to captivate and satisfy desire; for desire is truly infinite, having nothing less than God Himself for its origin and its end. One sees then—in a kind of paradox—that when the will seems to struggle against desire, it is not because desire is an evil inclination to be destroyed, but because it arrests a deeper movement which reaches out to infinity and can never be satisfied by any finite object. Every desire except the desire for God must lead to disillusionment. Only the desire for God is certain of fulfilment, for desire then is indistinguishable from love. The will no longer resists desire but becomes wedded to it, finding rest and repose in a fulfilment so intimate as to leave no room for will.

But does not this same antagonism between will and desire which appears to be for us a psychological law exist also between will and love? Should we not say in fact that the will is that part of ourselves which accepts responsibility for our fate; while love on the other hand is a power of attraction exercised by the object of our love, depending merely on our sensitive nature, that is on our aptitude to feel and respond to the attraction? Now this very sensibility is a gift which varies in different individuals. How is it possible to quicken love where it is mute: and how transmute into love the hostility or the hatred our senses sometimes feel? It is true that love cannot be created; and our very effort to

8

make good its absence makes this absence seem even more complete and irremediable. Take the fundamental precept of the Christian religion: 'Thou shalt love thy neighbour as thyself'. This simple command to love urges us through an act of our will to direct towards others the love of ourselves which is a law of all human nature. Is not this a species of challenge which, if met and answered, will transfuse our whole life with supernatural light?

We do well to approach the consideration of will and love at one and the same time; of will, which resides uniquely in an activity proper to us, and which is the very centre of our being, making us what we are—an activity that no other person can exercise in our place; and of love on the other hand, which is like a gift that is bestowed on us. By such a gift, instead of being enclosed within ourselves, we become united with another person and in principle even with Absolute Being with whom our existence is bound up and in whose Being we do no more than participate. Love transports us beyond ourselves; it is like an inspiration that is constantly being renewed, a power that is always present, sustaining us. But does not will also oblige us to go out of ourselves as though we found nothing within us that was capable of satisfying us? And, inversely, is it not we who love? And must we not therefore say that love reveals our secret essence and even the very heart of our being? For is it possible to will anything if we do not first love it? And where love is present, do we not in the very act of willing pass beyond will as if it were transcended and no longer needed? But must there not be within us a point at which our most profound act of will passes into love in its most hidden depth? In periods of aridity, when we can only make acts of will without any feeling of love for the object of our willing, our will tries of its own strength to supply the love that is lacking. It is a kind of imitation or quest of love. But when, in times of crisis, the will fights against love and resists it, what happens (when only the love of the senses is involved) is that the will invokes and seeks to be united to infinite love; and, when divine grace is involved, the will seeks to identify itself with the first impulses of love, and to fix them on the particular objects of its desire.

It is then from love that the will receives its strength, and from the will that love derives its weakness; and now we can see what is the bond uniting them. Will is nothing without love, for by love it is set in motion and stirred to action: without love it would be powerless. For what end could it set before itself, if it were of its nature indifferent to that end? How then could it rouse itself from inactivity? Whence could it derive even the possibility of constant renewal it possesses? The will in fact borrows from love all the strength it has at its command; though it has the power to use and discipline that strength. And so we see how the will, in an eager pursuit of enjoyment, sometimes devotes its whole attention to created things, forgetting that in these things there is nothing worthy of love except the act of love which created them; while at other times it gives rein to all the powers of love, and mounts beyond created things to the Infinite Source of Love, the abiding principle of their life and unity. It is not enough to say that we can create nothing save through love; we must go further and say that to love is to co-operate in the very act of creation. And this is the reason why it is the same thing to love God who is love and to love our neighbour as ourself, that is to say with the identical love by which God calls us both, our neighbour and ourselves, into existence.

We are now able to solve all the difficulties that are raised about the impossibility of loving at all, and the contradiction that is said to be inherent in the expression 'the will to love'. For love is the very heart of our existence, the stuff of our being. It is through an act of love that we come into existence and are endowed with the power to love. How can we explain our attachment to life in general and to our own individual life except through our love for the Supreme Being by whom we are caught up and with whom we are always co-operating? It should therefore not surprise us that love, which is our very essence, appears sometimes to come from outside as a gift bestowed on us; while at other times it seems to be born within us, though it seeks an abiding city elsewhere. It is not merely that love is the living principle of the universe of creatures; it is also because self can only find itself by putting off and by transcending its own limits. It is incapable of a separate existence, and it can only truly be said to be in itself when it has gone forth from itself; for its centre can be nothing less than the centre of the universe. Love consists precisely in that interior movement by which we seek ourselves by escaping from ourselves, and find ourselves by losing ourselves. We realize the intimacy of our self-awareness only in our awareness of all that transcends us. We identify the source of our own existence with the common source of all other existing things; and attain the perfection of our freedom in our affirmation of the whole work of creation, that is of the first creative act.

But love is not love unless we make it ours by an act of which the accomplishment depends on us. The will, which can never be a substitute for love, must discover and adhere to its object; otherwise love would never be wholly ours. Every soul must enter into the depths of love and make love its own. Love must ever be sought and willed, and it will continue to be an obscure and inoperative power within us until we turn our inward glance upon it. Those who complain that they cannot love are those who are content to remain on the surface of life, allowing themselves to be diverted by the outward appearances of things; or those who,

being immured in the cavern of their own conceit, are content to know nothing of the infinite reality of love save
through impulses at once extinguished by *amour propre*.
There is in the will an aspiration towards self-sufficiency; it
may be unaware of love or even despise it; although it is
love which sustains the will in all, even the least of those
activities which lead it to suppose it can take the place of love.
It may happen too, when love has won the contest, that the
will may fail to recognize its proper presence, for the will so
espouses its activity as to identify itself with it. But the things
we desire most ardently are those we love most deeply.
When love is absent, the will is incapable of action and de-
prived of efficacy: it is a power without activity. Yet without
will, love would be like an instinct or a grace imposing its
law on us without our being able to turn it into an act proper
to us—an act issuing from the depths of our personal being
and character and engaging our attention and responsibility.
Yet we recognize ourselves less in the acts of will we exert
than in the love we experience. All our mental effort is
directed towards the establishment of a harmony between
our acts of will and of love. The proper work of the will is
in the ordering of our love; for the will dictates the consent
or the refusal we give to love. It regulates the course of love
and must be vigilant to keep its flame alive and prevent it
from being diverted to objects which may allure but can
never satisfy it. Such objects are worthy of being loved only
in the light of the Infinite Love which sustains the will itself
and in which, once found, it reaches fulfilment.

III

Such is, for St. Francis de Sales, the meaning of that love
of God which may be said to include within itself all other
forms of love; and which instead of discrediting these other
forms, justifies their existence and supplies their rule of

action. There is, it is true, a *love of cupidity* that looks only for gain; but it is a love which we have caught and diverted from its proper end. True love, on the contrary, is a *love of benevolence*; our love for others must be either for the good they already possess, or for the good we bring to them. Love is always disinterested: 'it draws out the self' and transforms it into the object loved. We love God for Himself and not for our own sake, that 'His kingdom may come'. To live and to love are all one, for to love is to create; and he who loves can only will and create that which is good. Now it is because love comes from God and returns to Him that it bears within itself the character of infinity: to grow is of its essence. This is the obvious explanation of the paradox in St. Matthew [1]: 'If a man is rich, gifts will be made to him, and his riches will abound; if he is poor, even the little he has will be taken from him'.

It is of the nature of love to bridge the gap which separates finite beings one from another. And how can it do so save by bridging the other gap which separates each one from the Infinite Being who gives existence and life to all? For love is always one with its object, while desire continually pursues an ever-receding end. Love is the atmosphere in which the soul breathes, the space wherein it moves, the garden of paradise where man was not able to dwell. It is like a desire forever renewed and never sated by fulfilment: 'a desire that is always content and a contentment that is always desired'.

Yet love is born in us with desire. The soul may be said to have at once 'the desire for love and the love of desire'. Like desire love is a wound, a painful incision through which it flows away, like the precious resin called myrrh. Jesus, through love, became sorrowful unto death; and He has taught us that love fulfils itself in sacrifice. But the wound love makes in our flesh opens a way through which all the

[1] xiii. 12.

passions may enter. If love cannot be separated from desire, it must at least remove its sting. Love alone can bring peace of heart, which does not mean the absence of all desire, but the ability always to find the presence within us of the object of our desire. This can only be true of the love of God and of all things in God.

Love is the very life of our heart. 'And even as the weights give movement to all the mobile parts of a clock, so does love give its impulse to all the movements of the soul.' And again: 'All our affections follow our love'. We know that for St. Francis de Sales affection alone has value. Or rather for him as for some modern thinkers, it is affection, precisely as it proceeds from love, which weighs and measures the worth of all created things. For all things in the world are no more than occasions, vehicles, instruments or symbols of love. Love itself is the secret of souls, a dialogue without words which never ceases, and which only they who love have ears to hear. Those who love one another do not differ in outward showing from those who are indifferent; their actions are like those of everyone else; their speech is commonplace or insignificant. But their words have an interior echo to which all other ears are deaf and which has reality for them alone. They seem to shroud their very conversation in silence so that they alone can hear it. Far from seeking to leave their mark on the things that surround them, they seem to pass through them without leaving even a trace. Outward appearances fade away, leaving only their meaning behind. The interest of lovers is in the things that lie beyond: their life is in a universe of the spirit—a world invisible. For them the world of things has virtually ceased to be; its existence is known only through certain intimations not sensed by others, by which they are stirred and transported into a paradise where their souls delight in their proper essence as though they were no longer bound and imprisoned by the body.

The world itself is no more than the birthplace and the cradle of love. But love always has God for its object. It follows that in love all the powers of the soul come into action and commingle. When love acts in the understanding it begets contemplation, but when it acts in the will it begets communion. Our sole task therefore must be to found the practice of all our virtues and our actions on the principle of love alone. Love unites all our interior powers and does away with the need for their separate action, which is no longer of any avail, for love crowns and fulfils that effort on another plane. Love dwells in the 'fine point of the soul'. We know the use that has been made since the days of St. Francis de Sales of this concept of the fine point of the soul, where self, now exercising its most rarefied activity, ceases to be a power divided against itself, and is rid of all the preoccupations and cares that had hitherto occupied its attention. It is now able at a single bound to go beyond the world. But at the fine point of the soul, which lacks material dimension, and where love must rule, what can constitute the perfect act we ask of it save only simple consent to the gift that has been offered? Here is perhaps the essence of the act of love. 'What hast thou that thou hast not received?'[1] From God we have received even the power to consent to His gifts. Our co-operation has its source in the working of His grace and our free will acting together, and our freedom consists rather in the ability to withhold our consent than to give it. Hence the experience that each of us has had throughout our life, namely that we seem to be doing least when in reality we are doing most. Hence also that paradox so often to be found in the teaching of St. Francis de Sales when he invites us to sleep the sleep of love in perfect tranquillity of soul. When one who is at prayer becomes conscious that he is praying, it is clear that he is no longer recollected in his prayer; in the same way

[1] I Cor. iv. 7 (Douay).

perfect love is not conscious of itself and takes no delight in itself. Samson, whose name was 'Strength', was never conscious of the supernatural strength with which God endowed him at times. God never does anything in vain: He gives us strength and courage only when we are in need of them. The important thing is not that we should be conscious of such gifts but that we should make the right use of them. We must even learn to distinguish between God Himself and our awareness of Him. One who is about to suffer martyrdom is not necessarily thinking of God even at such a moment.

IV

It is especially this interior peace that St. Francis would have us strive to achieve; for it is the sign of our union with God—a sign not of inertia but of strength of soul. The ideals he exalts are precisely those most needed in our day: those we have perhaps ceased any longer to pursue. He seeks to root out from our souls the anxiety that some are inclined to treat as the essence of our self-hood, of an isolated being whose will is to rely only on itself though it finds in itself nothing but reasons for despair. The sole concern of St. Francis is to relieve our suffering and to help us to endure it; while modern thinkers seek rather to accentuate the bitterness of life and to prove that our suffering is in fact unendurable. By stressing our suffering such thinkers imagine they exalt us: to accept the least consolation, they tell us, would be to compromise our dignity. Even the union of the soul with God is said to be made in fear and anguish as though we were ready to repeat the primitive avowal: 'Of what use is any God to us unless we fear Him?' But this is to overlook the fact that the evolution of all religious thought, in the history both of the human race and of the individual consists precisely in the transformation of a God we fear into a

God we love: a God in whom all fear is cast out, except the
fear which is born of love.

But how are we to arrive at this perfect peace of soul
which is the very mark of the presence of God? No one
possesses it naturally and it is far from easy to attain. It can
only be achieved by an interior discipline which we must be
careful to practise. Must we then despise those whose souls
are untroubled? We must first ascertain whether their calm
is due to a lack of sensibility; or whether their sensibility is
sustained by a love so active and buoyant that nothing can
disturb it. It is surprising that St. Francis should urge us so
strongly to cultivate detachment, and that he should relate
detachment so closely to love as to make them seem indistinguishable. Yet there is a species of detachment which is at the
same time the instrument and the effect of love; for we must
love nothing save the will of God; and in relation to His will
all particular things are matters of indifference. All we are
bidden to do is 'not to violate the law of detachment in
things which are themselves indifferent'. We must seek to
dissolve our will in the will of God, for it is through the
dissolution of our own will that we achieve detachment.
The heart of one whose will is wholly united to the will of
God has no longer any occasion to make a choice. He is of
all men the most detached; and as St. John of the Cross has
taught us, he who is most detached is at the same time most
rich: possessing nothing, he possesses all things.

But we cannot so order things that our bodies shall not
be a burden, and that our passions shall not stir in us, and that
our individual will shall not habitually set itself against the
will of God. That has been the condition of our nature since
the Fall; and we must accordingly learn to accept and endure
it. When we are distressed by our lack of perfection it is to
be feared that pride may often be the cause of our distress.
'Our grief that we are imperfect springs not so much from

love of God as from love of ourselves.' This is why 'some
souls are so busy thinking about what they have to do that
they never have time to do anything'. There is in us a life
according to nature and a life according to the spirit—that is
the life of grace. The opposition between these two lives
needs to be eliminated, so that the life of nature, instead of
being an obstacle, may become a means to the life of grace.
We must learn to be patient in regard to those events which
do not depend upon us and are merely transient. There is in
us a state of attention, which is an act of the will—a readiness
to accept whatever may happen. In our interior life we must
learn to accept periods of aridity and of consolation, of
tedium and dejection, as well as periods of spiritual insight
and progress, for all help us equally to forget ourselves and
to put all our hope in God. We must ask nothing and refuse
nothing, and put this precept into practice even in our suffering. And in regard to our passions we must not be cast down
when we feel their assault within us; for all depends on our
attitude towards them. It is vain to try and get rid of them:
our duty is to control and make use of them (and here we
have a foreshadowing of Cartesian thought). We are not
masters of the movements of nature; we cannot prevent our
emotions from rising within us, or restrain the blood from
mounting to our cheeks; that measure of control we shall
never achieve. But in the fine point of our soul we must
always preserve a pure intention; and when passion or prejudice makes itself felt in the interior part of our soul
'we must pay no more attention than passers-by would do
to dogs barking in the distance'. Flashes of pride must simply
be ignored: we cannot repel them by 'force of arms'. And
speaking broadly 'when we reach a point where discord is
inevitable, we must not break the strings but relax the tension
when we become conscious of dissonance; and give ear to
detect the source of disharmony, tightening or slackening the

strings as our art enjoins'. To accept the situation in which we find ourselves is the very condition of our spiritual life. We must be content to remain willingly and at peace in the barque in which God has placed us to make the journey from this world to the next. 'We must certainly hate our faults, not in a spirit of resentment and agitation, but in tranquillity and peace of mind.' All devotion is false which is not suited to our state of life. 'Be prepared to find weeds growing in your soul and be ready to root them out, for as long as life lasts pride will never be entirely cast out. . . . Is it not better to have thorns as well as roses in our garden than to have no roses in order to have no thorns?'

We must always strive to attain tranquillity and be pre-pared to sacrifice everything rather than our peace of mind. 'This is the remedy I prescribe, and I always forbid excessive zeal'; for such excessive zeal is an effect of pride. Pride may even insinuate itself into humility, which should be simple and peaceful, and never fretful or agitated. We should avoid excess of vigilance, for this interrupts the spontaneity of our natural movements and is a sign of self-seeking rather than piety. Nor should we worry unduly over the outcome of our actions but always leave the issue in the hands of God. We must not strive to do more than we are able and must always be patient with ourselves, bearing with our imperfections as a means to perfection, 'keeping our heart detached and free, not driving it too hard towards some good which is perhaps beyond our strength. . . . Why build castles in Spain if we have to live in France? . . . How foolish are those who dream of being martyred in the Indies and yet neglect their duty in the state of life to which they have been called.' It is also good to avoid subtleties and to tackle boldly each thing as it comes; for most of our troubles are more imaginary than real. Faith and trust are all one; and the humility which makes us conscious of our ineffectiveness has its counterpart in 'the generosity which assures us we can do everything in Him who strengthens us'. Why spend time worrying over some misfortune that may never happen? And even if it does happen, God will always give us the help and inspiration we need. 'Man is like a little child in leading-strings who can never make a false step or suffer hurt if he throws himself into the arms of God; for God will always bear him up and embrace him in His love.' It is unreasonable to think that sin can have as much power against charity as charity has against sin. And in our worst sorrows and failures we must still hold fast to 'the supreme consolation that the will of God is always done'.

v

Such is the doctrine of St. Francis de Sales in which will and love are distinguished one from the other only to be united. Love is will directed to what is right, though its capacity to err must always remain if it is to deserve the name of will. And without this presence of will in the very heart of love, our responsibility and even our personality would be abolished. There is in us a true 'monarchy' of the will. God would seem to have spoken to the will as Pharaoh spoke to Joseph: 'Thou shalt have charge of my household and all my people shall obey thy word of command. No one shall move without thy permission.'[1] But the will changes its quality according to the love with which it is united; for there is a unity in love which stretches from man to God and from the material to the spiritual. It is right for us to love even our bodies since they are part of our person and the condition of our spiritual life. Our natural inclinations must not be thwarted but sublimated. Now if the love of God is the latest in the order of time among all the affections of the human heart (for St. Paul tells us that

[1] Gen. xli. 40, 44.

'natural life came first, then spiritual life'[1]), this late-comer inherits all authority, and is cherished and obeyed not only by all the other inclinations of the soul but also by the understanding and the will. It is therefore a good sign when virtue perfects our nature and does not constrain it. Virtue always takes natural inclinations as its instruments and transfigures them. We find St. Francis de Sales using similes borrowed from nature to symbolize the movements of grace; for these movements have their beginning in nature, where the soul starts on its return to God. On this point St. Francis de Sales differs widely from St. Francis of Assisi for whom the created world is the immediate revelation of the countenance of God, the infinite and ever-present goodness of the creative act.

But though there is continuity between human and divine love, we realize the distance there is between loving God through the love of a human being, and loving a human being through our love of God; and between loving God for His own sake, and loving ourselves because of God and because we are made in the image of God. Love is like a return to the very source of our existence. It is the perfection of our will, the point where our will reaches its fulfilment and is dissolved in the will of God. 'Our free will is never so free as when it is a slave of the will of God, and is never so arrogant as when it serves our own will; never has it such fullness of life as when it dies to itself, and never is it so near to death as when it lives only for self.' We need not be surprised to find that in its own development the will must endeavour to elicit love; that its sole task must be to increase the measure of its love; it must do nothing save for love, and all its labour and even death must proceed from love. But how can the will elicit love unless it first receives it in the form of grace? Love is only another name for grace itself to

[1] I Cor. xv. 46.

which the will needs only to consent. Will is the only road leading us from nature to grace. And it is easy to understand why love is defined as 'the weight of everything', and why it is always gentle, effortless, spiritual, serene and hidden, and why the law is 'not made for the just man' as St. Paul says, for love is already in him. With love it must be all or nothing. Love knows neither prisoners nor slaves. It is an infinity whose possession is always beyond us and which ought to fill us not with uneasiness but with admiration. As each new day dawns we ought to feel a thrill of joy at the thought of yet another day in which to love God. 'Night is as day when God is in our heart; but when He is absent day is as night.'